NEW SWAN SHAKESPEARE

GENERAL EDITOR
BERNARD LOTT, M.A.

*

Twelfth Night

NEW SWAN SHAKESPEARE

WILLIAM SHAKESPEARE

Twelfth Night

EDITED BY

BERNARD LOTT, M.A.

LONGMAN

LONGMAN GROUP UK LIMITED
*Longman House, Burnt Mill, Harlow,
Essex CM20 2JE, England
and Associated Companies throughout the world.*

First published 1959
Second edition 1965
Reprinted 1986

ISBN 0-582-52715-5

Illustrations by Clyde Pearson

Cover illustration by Caroline Holmes-Smith

We are indebted to the Southern Universities Joint Board
and the Welsh Joint Education Committee for permission
to reproduce past examination questions.

Produced by Longman Singapore Publishers Pte Ltd.
Printed in Singapore

INTRODUCTION

The purpose of this book is to give the text of Shakespeare's play *Twelfth Night* and to explain it in the simplest way. The text itself is Shakespeare's own, complete, not simplified or shortened, although the spelling has been modified. Shakespeare's stage directions (SD), indicating actors' movements, the introduction of music and noises, etc., have been made clearer than they are in the original text, and added to as necessary.

The text is explained by notes on the opposite pages. The presence of a note is signalled in the text by a small number above the word or phrase in question. These notes are kept as simple as possible. They are written within the range of a list of the 3,000 most commonly used English words, with a few added; the meanings of these extra words should be clear from the way they are used, and you will need them when you come to discuss the play.

Words in the play itself which are outside the 3,000-word vocabulary but which are still used with the same meaning in modern English are not necessarily explained in the notes. For such words you may need to use a dictionary such as the *Longman Dictionary of Contemporary English,* which explains them using a limited vocabulary of 2,000 words.

The rest of this introduction is arranged under the following headings:

1 The Story of Twelfth Night

Sebastian and Viola, who are twins and look very like each other, are shipwrecked and thrown ashore at separate places on the coast of Illyria, each believing that the other is drowned. Viola disguises herself as a boy, calling herself Cesario, and becomes a page in the service of Orsino, the Duke of Illyria. She falls in love with him. He, however, wishes to marry the lady Olivia, and sends "Cesario" to try to persuade her to accept him; but Olivia falls in love with the supposed page instead. While exploring the town, Sebastian is followed by his friend and rescuer, the sea-captain Antonio; but just as Antonio comes upon Viola, whom he takes for Sebastian, he is arrested as an old enemy by Orsino's officers.

Later, Olivia persuades Sebastian to marry her, believing him to be "Cesario", and at last, when brother and sister appear together, the mistakes are explained, and Viola marries the Duke Orsino.

Meanwhile, Sir Toby Belch, Olivia's uncle, his companion Sir Andrew Aguecheek and the maid Maria play a trick on Malvolio, the lady's steward. They send him a letter which he takes to be a loveletter from Olivia; in it he is recommended to dress and act in a strange way in order to win her love. When he does so he is treated as a madman, and much fun is made of him by Feste, Olivia's clown, and Fabian, her servant.

2 The Language

The English of Shakespeare's time was in many ways different from the English we speak today. A number of words or parts of words are listed below which are seldom used today as Shakespeare used them, but which occur so often in the play that it would waste space to explain them every time they appear. These words have either changed in meaning since Shakespeare's day, or fallen out of use altogether in everyday modern English, or are shortened forms which Shakespeare used for some special effect, e.g. so as to fit in with the metrical pattern of the lines.

(No attempt should be made to learn this list by heart; it is to be consulted when difficulties occur which are not explained in the notes.)

an – (sometimes, particularly at the beginning of sentences) "if".

anon – "at once".

ay – "yes".

but – (sometimes) "only".

cousin, coz – any close relative (not necessarily the child of an uncle or aunt).

do, does, did are often used with another verb and without adding any separate meaning; e.g. ". . . after our ship *did* split" (I.ii.8).

e'er – "ever".

'em – "them".

faith or *i' faith* – "in faith, indeed", an exclamation.

fie – an exclamation expressing disgust.

forth – "forward and out".

haply – "perhaps".

hence – "from this place".

hither – "to this place".

hold! – "stop! look!"

how now! – "hallo! oh! what news?"

knave – "dishonest man, boy".

marry! – "(By the Virgin) Mary!", an exclamation.

methinks – "it seems to me".

mine – (sometimes) "my".

nay – "no".

needs – "necessarily".

ne'er – "never".

o' – "of".

o'er – "over".

on – (sometimes) "of", e.g. *on 't* – "of it".

perchance – "perhaps".

prithee – "I pray thee; please".

sirrah – a form of address used to servants.

sooth – "truth".

still – (sometimes) "always".

't – "it".

-th is the usual ending for verb-forms of the third person singular present indicative; e.g. "she that *hath* a heart" (I.i.32).

thou, thee, thy, thine – "you, your, yours" (singular).

These words are often used for the second person singular pronoun. The verb associated with the subject *thou* ends in *-est* or *-st*, e.g. *Know'st thou* this country? (I.ii.19).

The verb *to be* and a few others are, however, irregular in this respect, e.g.

O spirit of love! how quick and fresh *art thou* (I.i.9).

Thou hast spoke for us (I.v.98).

troth in the phrase *by my troth* – "indeed".

whence – "from which place".

whither – "to which place".

would – often means "wish", "I wish".

yond – "that".

yonder – "over there".

Like all poets, Shakespeare employed language in a way which is not usual for the making of direct statements in prose. A great deal of what he wrote is not prose but verse. The lines of verse he puts into the mouths of his characters generally follow a fixed pattern of stressed and unstressed syllables; e.g.:

> How éasy ís it f'ó'r the próper-fálse
> In wómen's wáxen héarts to sét their fórms (II.ii.26-7)

in which the rhythm depends upon five stressed syllables in each line. This is, in fact, the usual arrangement, but completely regular rhythm (which would be dull to listen to) is avoided by varying the positions of the stressed syllables in the lines, or by making a rhythmic stress fall lightly on an unaccented syllable, as on *for* in the first of the lines given above. Occasionally the lines rhyme in couplets (i.e. two lines next to one another), particularly at the end of a scene or of a long speech of a character within a scene.

The poetic use of language is also characterised by imagery, which adds to ordinary statements visions of something different, but at the same time similar in some respects. Imagery may be expressed by the use of simile or metaphor.

A *simile* is a direct comparison between the subject treated and the image that subject recalls; e.g.:

> That strain . . .
>   . . . came o'er my ear like the sweet sound
> That breathes upon a bank of violets. (I.i.4-6)

The strain of music which feeds the Duke's passion is directly compared with the gentle wind that blows over a bank of spring flowers.

A *metaphor* is a comparison which is only suggested, not made directly. Words used metaphorically refer at once to two or more different things, usually recalled together in a moment of strong feeling. Orsino says, in the lines quoted above:

> the sweet sound
> That *breathes* upon a bank of violets,

thinking of the wind making a sound and also of the wind "breathing" as if it came from a living body. Some critics have said that only a living being can breathe, and have changed the lines accordingly. But Shakespeare was not here dealing with the facts of observed science; his purpose was to express the wishes and feelings of a nobleman in love.

The effect of an image in a Shakespeare play is heightened by the awareness that certain ideas run through the whole imagery of the play, binding it organically as the plot does. In *Twelfth Night* there is, for example, a pattern of imagery referring to hunting; this begins with a play on the words *heart* and *hart*, the lover being thought of as a huntsman:

Curio.   Will you go hunt, my lord?
Duke.   What, Curio?
Curio.   The hart.
Duke.   Why, so I do, the noblest that I have.
          Oh, when mine eyes did see Olivia first . . .
          That instant was I turned into a hart.   (I.i.16–20)

A little later, the image is extended to include Cupid's arrow and a "flock" of affections:

          How will she love, when the rich golden shaft
          Hath killed the flock of all affections else
          That live in her . . .! (I.i.34–6)

When Olivia at last declares her love for "Cesario", and then, seeing it is hopeless, tries to throw it off, she thinks of animals preying upon human beings:

          If one should be a prey, how much the better
          To fall before the lion than the wolf! (III.i.119–20)

Later when Olivia stops Sebastian ("Cesario" as she thinks) from continuing a fight with Sir Toby and Sir Andrew, she says to him:

          Beshrew his soul for me,
          He started one poor heart of mine in thee (IV.i.51–2)

thus returning to the *heart/hart* pun of the beginning.

Twelfth Night is not as full of imagery as a great deal of Shakespeare's work, partly because so much of it is in prose, whereas imagery is particularly associated with poetry.

Verse is generally used by the nobler people, particularly at times of strong feeling. Prose is used by the humbler and the comic characters, and by others when their feelings are less strong. Orsino seldom speaks in prose. He does so in conversation with Feste (V.i.6 ff.), but as soon as his feelings are stirred, Antonio being brought before him, he speaks in verse again. By contrast, Sir Toby never speaks in verse except when, having drunk too much, he breaks into snatches of popular songs (e.g. at II.iii.73 ff.). The nobler characters tend to use metaphors in their speech:

Duke.   . . . Come, boy, with me; my thoughts are ripe in
          mischief;
          I'll sacrifice the lamb that I do love,
          To spite a raven's heart within a dove. (V.i.120-2)

The humbler characters seem more often to use similes:

Sir Toby. And cross-gartered?
Maria.   Most villainously; like a pedant that keeps a school i'
          the church. I have dogged him like a murderer. He
          . . . does smile his face into more lines than is in the
          new map with the augmentation of the Indies.
                                                   (III.ii.61-6)

Perhaps only Feste, who seems to be lord of this comedy, moves easily between the two:

     Lady, *cucullus non facit monachum*: that's as much to say as I
     wear not motley in my brain. (I.v.48-9)

3 The Play as Drama

Twelfth Night, or What You Will was very probably written for performance on the "Twelfth Night", i.e. the last night of the Christmas holiday, January 6th, in the year 1601. It is also likely that it was first presented before Queen Elizabeth I in a great hall of her palace of Whitehall, just outside London. The play would suit such an occasion, since it is a delightful, lighthearted comedy, full of love and laughter, and with only a cloud or two to pass across the happy sunshine.

What we have before us here, then, is not essentially a book at all, but the words of a play, something which was written to be spoken with action. For a fully successful reading, the student must keep this fact in mind, and take every opportunity of speaking the lines aloud rather than reading them silently. We cannot all be actors, nor have we all the time or ability to learn long speeches, but we can, perhaps, read parts together, or stage some striking scenes (even if this means acting with book in hand), and in doing this try to imagine the play as it might appear in the theatre.

One cannot go very far in such a living presentation of the play without realizing that the theatre for which it was written differed in some ways from that of our own day. When *Twelfth Night* was first performed, it was probably staged in the middle of the great hall, with simple scenery placed there for the play, and entirely surrounded by the audience, though the actors acted for the most part in the direction of the queen herself. In the public theatres the stage stretched far out into the open space where the audience sat or stood – so far, in fact, that they were gathered round three sides of it. The fourth side extended back a considerable way, forming a recess which was roofed over by a second floor. This arrangement made it very easy for one or more players to act in close contact with the audience, leaving others, when necessary, in the background. In this way the foolery of Maria's plot to deceive Malvolio could be commented on by her, Sir Toby, and the others, all hidden behind the box-tree, while Malvolio himself would appear too far away to notice them (II.v). Again, Malvolio might be confined to the recess, and curtains drawn across to close him in when he was tricked into appearing mad (IV.ii).

Since public theatres were normally unroofed, no stage lighting was possible, and as far as is known very little scenery was used, although the private theatres had movable wooden "houses" which could, in *Twelfth Night*, for example, represent Olivia's and Orsino's palaces, one on either side of the open space. Shakespeare wrote his play for the simple stages of Elizabethan times, making it move fast and giving impressions from the speech of his characters which make, say, the trees of a garden or the hangings of a state room seem quite unnecessary.

4 *The Construction of the Play*

There are two main plots. In the first, Orsino, who is in love with Olivia, woos her through a messenger, Viola, whom he believes to be a boy named Cesario. Olivia falls in love with "Cesario"; the true Viola loves the Duke. Her twin brother, exactly like her in outward appearance, unwittingly resolves this hopeless situation by being persuaded to marry Olivia, leaving Viola free to marry Orsino.

In the second plot, Malvolio, Olivia's steward, is tricked by her uncle and her maid-servant (Sir Toby and Maria) into believing that she is in love with him; as a result of this he behaves so strangely that he is taken to be mad and locked up. Sir Toby and the others mock him but he wins Olivia's sympathy in the end.

The link between these two plots is outwardly the relationship between Olivia and (on the one hand) her steward Malvolio, and (on the other) her lover Orsino. More deeply, the play is bound together by these stories each being an example of normal life turned upside-down: in everyday life a girl does not disguise herself as a boy, particularly when she has a twin brother who looks very like her; not does a servant in a lady's household, however important his position may be, allow himself to be easily led into believing that the lady is in love with him.

The end of the play shows which of the plots is more important: it is Olivia, Sebastian, Viola, and Orsino who are left happily settled. Malvolio has played his part in their affairs, and leaves the play with nothing more than a threat that he will be revenged on the whole pack of them

The comedy situations, e.g. at II.v.24 ff., where Malvolio picks up and reads the mock love-letter, sometimes depend for the greater part of their effect on an accepted stage practice (convention) by which the audience can hear all the actors, but they are imagined not always to be able to hear one another. When Malvolio finds the letter, his deceivers hide behind a box-tree and make loud remarks on what is happening. It is to be imagined that Malvolio cannot hear them; but the audience can, and they can also hear Malvolio speaking his thoughts and reading his letter. In the same way Sir Toby encourages both Viola and Sir Andrew to start fighting one another, but neither can hear the other's conversation until they are actually face-to-face and ready for the duel (III.iv.253 ff.). This practice was perhaps more acceptable on the stage for which Shakespeare wrote than it can be in the modern theatre, for, as we have seen, actors were then in closer contact with the audience than they can usually be today.

Another accepted practice used in the play is that of disguise. The audience was prepared to imagine that a change of dress was enough to make one character unable to recognize another, even though he knew him well. The trick of disguise is used in *Twelfth Night*, and it can be seen in various earlier plays from which Shakespeare took ideas – some old Italian plays, a comedy of the Roman dramatist Plautus, and, earlier still, a certain type of Greek play. This explains why Sebastian, meeting his sister at last, fails to recognize her at once because she is dressed in boy's clothes such as would, in the theatre, be exactly like his own; Antonio says,

> An apple, cleft in two, is not more twin
> Than these two creatures. Which is Sebastian? (V.i.208–9)

Another dramatic trick, and one which continues to amuse audiences today, is that of a character saying things which have more meaning for the audience than they have for the speaker himself; this is called *dramatic irony*. It can be seen that disguise readily brings dramatic irony, for a speaker who mistakes the identity of someone can say things to him meaning one thing to the speaker but much more to the spectators who know the truth about the other character. There is good dramatic irony in Orsino's speech to Viola (I.iv.29 ff.), in which he gives his reasons for thinking that she will woo Olivia successfully for him. The audience know that Viola is a girl dressed to look like a page, but Orsino does not. Yet he says:

> they shall yet belie thy happy years
> That say thou art a man; Diana's lip
> Is not more smooth and rubious; thy small pipe
> Is as the maiden's organ, shrill and sound,
> And all is semblative a woman's part. (I.iv.29–33)

Here *Diana*, *maiden's organ*, *woman's part* bring out the dramatic irony of the passage.

Similarly, Malvolio reports on the arrival of Viola at Olivia's house in a way which is more meaningful to the audience (who know that the page is no boy at all) than to either of the speakers:

Olivia.	What kind o' man is he?
Malvolio.	Why, of mankind.
Olivia.	What manner of man?
Malvolio.	Of very ill manner; he 'll speak with you, will you or no. (I.v.132–5)

These are some of the ways in which the play moves us to smiling or to laughter. We are looking at a world turned upside-down, which is just as it should be in a play for Twelfth Night, since during that Night it used to be the custom for young people to dress up and make fun of the habits of their elders. A "Lord of Misrule" led the Twelfth Night entertainments, when the high were brought low and the humble became, for a few hours, the important people. Shakespeare's audiences would know the custom and might see in Feste a delightful Lord of Misrule, ruling this strange world for a short time. And although he is, we may well believe, an old man, most of the characters are young, and make the comedy fresh and happy. Yet the treatment of Malvolio in his dark room is never an object of laughter; few hearts can remain untouched by his earnest pleading:

> Good Sir Topas, do not think I am mad; they have laid me here in hideous darkness (IV.ii.24–5)

or be moved at the grandeur of his views on Pythagoras:

> I think nobly of the soul, and no way approve his opinion
> (IV.ii.45)

Even Sir Andrew, fool though he is, makes us pity him in his foolishness, for we know that in the hours when he is alone self-questionings must creep up on him, and he will at last be left lonely and without an audience for his well-worked stock of commonplace remarks.

> Youth 's a stuff will not endure (II.iii.46)

sings the clown; and although we need not take him too seriously, there is an air of sadness in *Twelfth Night*, usually faint and far-away but still to be sensed, which we do not find in Shakespeare's earlier comedies. This is some justification for thinking that the play was written immediately before the great tragedies, when Shakespeare's thoughts were taking a more serious turn. Other indications, too, suggest that *Twelfth Night* was written in or about 1600, to be followed by *Hamlet* a year later. But however true this may be, it should never be thought that the play is the worse for having an undercurrent of seriousness. Such a strain is present in the oldest classical comedies, and a plot can hardly exist without some sort of set-back; and there is no reason at all why, even in a comedy, this set-back should not be serious. Shakespeare wrote *Twelfth Night* at the height of his powers, and we must read his comedy prepared for deeper experience as well as the simpler pleasure of laughter.

5 The Characters

To study the most important characters in *Twelfth Night* is to observe different sorts of people under the influence of love. Orsino and Olivia are perhaps most nearly alike in this respect. Each is a clever and sensible person of high rank, yet in the play both act in a way which shows that they cannot fully command their good sense, since love has entrapped them.

Orsino was known to the Captain as "a noble duke, in nature as in name" (I.ii.23). He is a lover of music and poetry and the beauties of nature, and his passionate love for Olivia turns to the fulfilment of these pleasures. Although he is a faithful lover until he knows that his love is hopeless, he cannot take direct action; instead he stays at home to think of his love, and woos by messenger. It is this which gives him an opportunity to enjoy music and poetry; he even arranges for music to be played while he is telling "Cesario" of his sadness (II.iv.12 ff.), using beautiful poetry to do so. Yet he is perhaps less than fair to himself or his sex in saying that men are less firm in purpose than women are. For when there are affairs of state to be attended to, as with Antonio in V.i.42 ff., he is both firm and purposeful. When he sees that he has no hope of wooing Olivia successfully, he quickly decides that he will try to prevent her from fulfilling her own passion for "Cesario". He is then told that "Cesario" is already married to Olivia, but in reality it is Sebastian, not "Cesario", whom she has married. At the end of the play Orsino again takes on the duties of a noble lord, hearing arguments and judging between them as a man in his position was expected to do. He is practical enough, too, to see that Viola loves him dearly, and that when Olivia firmly rejects him it is Viola that he should choose as a wife. This change takes place very quickly, and with the prospect of a happy marriage he is able to throw off the uncertainty under which he feels he has suffered, and to assume once more the full power of his character and position.

Olivia is a noble lady, quick in understanding, witty in speech, and warm-hearted towards those around her. At the beginning of the play she seems too level-headed for the fancies of love to play tricks on her. She has made a vow to mourn for seven years the loss of her brother, and this she uses as an excuse for not seeing Orsino or listening to his messenger. But when that messenger gains admittance, and appears as the attractive "boy" Cesario, she, like Orsino, finds her affections changing more quickly than she had thought possible, and she falls in love with him. "Even so quickly may one catch the plague?" she asks herself.

Valentine, the Duke's servant, first explains Olivia's coldness and the reasons for her vow. She is tricked into appearing foolish when Feste questions her on it (I.v.54 ff.), but when "Cesario" appears she has enough common sense to confess to herself that she is in love with him; yet she keeps her head and speaks most wittily when Orsino's messenger arrives. At the same time her uncle, Sir Toby, is causing her a good deal of trouble, and she wisely attempts to control him and Sir Andrew through her maid Maria (II.iii.63). At the end of their second meeting, Olivia declares openly her love for "Cesario". Viola tells her indirectly that she cannot return this love, and the impossible situation is resolved by the arrival of Viola's twin brother Sebastian, a man indeed, and a quick and practical wooer who succeeds in gaining Olivia's love in a very short time. When she meets Orsino again, she is married, and learns who her husband really is. She has been deceived, but the end of the play shows that she has lost none of her humanity; for she treats Malvolio kindly and refuses to make fun of him when his foolishness over the love-letter is finally exposed.

Viola and Sebastian, together with Olivia and Orsino, make a cross-pattern of love. Separated in a shipwreck, these twins, exactly like each other in appearance, enter the affairs of love when Viola decides to serve the Duke Orsino. She soon finds herself in love with the Duke but must keep it secret because she is disguised as a boy. When Sebastian appears, Olivia mistakes him for Orsino's messenger

"Cesario", and he is very quickly married to her (IV.iii). This may seem improbable, but it is easier to believe when we remember that the women's parts in Shakespeare's plays were originally acted by boys dressed up to look like women. The boy who played Viola, dressed as a girl and then "disguised" as a boy, could look very like Sebastian, a boy all the time, and the complication of the duel could be seen as a result of natural misunderstanding.

Viola is like a fairly-tale princess. She is beautiful and clever; like Orsino, she often shows her feeling for the poetry of words; and her sincerity and deep feeling are revealed when she is at last able to declare her love for the Duke (V.i.125). Her courage and good sense almost desert her only when she is on the point of fighting a duel:

> A little thing would make me tell them how much I lack of a man. (III.iv.262 ff.)

With this can be compared her admirable humour when she turns the "conned" speech from Orsino into a delightful conversation with Olivia (I.v.149 ff.). Her reasons for deciding to serve the Duke as a page are not certain; but much of the interest of the play lies in watching Viola handling the situation she has placed herself in.

Sebastian serves as a contrast to the Duke. He is a man who wants to get things done, and is not the sort of person to stay at home thinking of the sweet sorrows of love. He is deeply moved by thoughts of his sister, whom he believes to be drowned, and wants to be alone; but Antonio is so much attracted to him that he determines to follow him, even at great risk to himself. They meet again near Orsino's house. Sebastian wants to see the sights of the town, and Antonio, because he is in danger, entrusts his money to him. From then on Sebastian is mistaken for "Cesario"; he treats the complications which arise from this in a very practical way, and in the end is happy to win in marriage no less a person than the rich and beautiful Olivia.

If *Twelfth Night* had been just a gay, light comedy, *Malvolio* could hardly have taken a part in it, for he is a character who experiences a downfall which is no laughing matter. His position as steward in Olivia's house gives him authority over the other servants and to some extent even over her uncle, Sir Toby. But his powers of leadership prove insufficient for this authority; he has too high an opinion of himself and too little understanding of others. He is therefore easily tricked by a letter into believing that his lady is in love with him (II.v.75 ff.) and he dresses and behaves as the letter advises him, without realising that he is being greatly deceived. He is, indeed, "sick of self-love" (I.v.78) and unable to laugh, least of all at himself; but he is a good steward, and Olivia wins much sympathy for him when she says:

> Alas! poor fool, how they have baffled thee! (V.i.350)

and earlier:

> Let some of my people have a special care of him: I would not have him miscarry for the half of my dowry. (III.iv.57)

He is imprisoned for madness and cruel fun is made of him, a hard punishment for the sickness of self-love, and at the end he is without regret, asking only for revenge (V.i.358).

Maria and Sir Toby have no such feelings about his downfall. Sir Toby, it is true, has some doubts about the way Malvolio is mocked, but these really arise only from fear for his own safety:

> If he may be conveniently delivered, I would he were; for I am now so far in offence with my niece that I cannot pursue with any safety this sport to the upshot. (IV.ii.57-9)

Malvolio's downfall serves to show how common and unfeeling both Maria and Sir Toby are.

Malvolio's letter to Olivia from prison is certainly not madness, as the Duke quickly sees (V.i.294), yet his over-serious concern for himself is enough to prevent us from feeling full of sympathy for him, especially if we think of him as a fairly young man too much aware of his position of authority and, without the right to be so, a proud judge of the behaviour of others. In the end we can forgive the bitterness of his treatment since we know in our hearts that he will never improve.

Sir Toby Belch, on the contrary, takes very little seriously, least of all himself. He represents a memory of a past age, when men who belonged to rich families could, if they liked, live in idleness, taking small interest in the daily affairs of their property and trusting to others for their livelihood. Sir Toby's constant drunkenness and noisiness are amusing on the stage, but they seldom provide a background for wit, so seldom in fact that even his best comic situation, his presence at Malvolio's day-dream wooing (II.v.19 ff.), is no more than lightly comic. Among the observers, indeed, it is Sir Toby who seems most heartless and cruel; he may have suffered most at the hands of this proud steward, or perhaps he simply fails to understand a person so different from himself. His part in the play is chiefly to help when others are being made to look foolish. Sir Andrew is deceived into thinking that Olivia is in love with him, and is to be wooed and won. Malvolio is tricked by a letter into acting and dressing foolishly in order to attract his lady. Feste pretends to be a parson and visits Malvolio in his dark room. Viola and Sir Andrew are each persuaded that the other wants a fight, and for his part in this Sir Toby is wounded in the head (V.i.165). In all this Sir Toby plays a leading part. He is unable to bring himself "within the modest limits of order", and one wonders whether even Maria would ever be able to make him change for the better.

One person has complete faith in Sir Toby; he is *Sir Andrew Aguecheek*, a fool so perfect that he becomes delightful in his foolishness. We laugh at him because he is warm and human in his stupidity, and because he has enough vanity for his deceivers to work upon very successfully, both in the big things of life (e.g. when he is persuaded that Olivia is secretly in love with him) and in the small things, as when he tries hard to appear an essential actor in the little jokes played on Malvolio:

> – Or o' mine either? . . .
> – I' faith, or I either? . . .
> – I 'll make one too . . . (II.v.160, 163, 176)

In his attempts to join in with the rest, poor Sir Andrew's best trick is to catch up other people's words. Sometimes, he does this consciously, as when he makes up his mind to remember the high-sounding words used by "Cesario" in her wooing of Olivia:

> "Odours", "pregnant", and "vouchsafed"; I 'll get 'em all three all ready (III.i.81-2)

At other times it is unconscious:

> *Sir Toby.* A contagious breath.
>
> *Sir Andrew.* Very sweet and contagious, i' faith; (II.iii.48–9)

or

> *Sir Toby.* She 's a beagle, true bred, and one that adores me;
> what o' that?
>
> *Sir Andrew.* I was adored once too.   (II.iii.153–4)

This happens frequently and makes Sir Andrew a shadow of the man he trusts; it leads him to express delight in word-play which he does not in the least understand, and to praise as "the best fooling, when all is done" (II.iii.26) what Feste intends to be complete nonsense.

Yet, because the joke must sooner or later turn against him, and his vanity is not sufficient to carry him through the anxiety of the duel, at the end there remains in him something lonely and helpless which must win our hearts, coward though he is:

> I had rather than forty pound I were at home. (V.i.164–5)

Feste is a good and amusing clown; "wise enough to play the fool", is what Viola says of him (III.i.52), and all she has to tell (in the lines which follow) of the duties of a good clown are just the things which Feste can do well. In fact, in this upside-down world of comedy, where the high-born characters, crossed in love, sometimes act like children, and the solemn, self-important Malvolio is humbled almost to madness, it is Feste who never loses his head, who sits astride this "whirligig of time" (V.i.356). Since his work is to amuse men, he has made man his special study, and can change his manner to suit many different sorts of people. He is a good character actor, as he shows when he plays the part of Sir Topas (IV.ii.11 ff.) which successfully deceives Malvolio; he is indeed "for all waters" (IV.ii.52), serious or comic, learned or nonsensical, the wit or the practical joker, just as the occasion seems to suggest. And he knows where his skill lies:

> Foolery, sir, does walk about the orb like the sun; it shines
> everywhere. (III.i.32–3)

Feste knows himself as well as he knows his fellow men. He calls himself a "corrupter of words" (III.i.30), since that suggests word-play, the sort of wit his age and his employer particularly wished to hear; he knows he can sing well, and in various styles; he even knows exactly how far he can go in his relationships with those he moves among; as he leaves Olivia in I.v. his respect for her is touched with just enough scorn for her uncle Sir Toby:

He is but mad yet, madonna; and the fool shall look to the madman. (I.v.120–1)

But he has no fear of Sir Andrew, and disrespectfully interrupts one of Sir Andrew's foolish remarks:

Sir Andrew. There's a testril of me too: if one knight give a –
Feste. Would you have a love-song, or a song of good life?
Sir Toby. A love-song, a love-song. (II.iii.29–31)

Since Feste once worked for Olivia's father, it is probably right to see him as a rather old man, boyish at times but having enough of the dignity of age to speak to the point when the circumstances are right.

Maria is more likely to be seen as young, full of life and small in size, the "youngest wren of nine" as Sir Toby calls her. She shares with Feste that quality of level-headedness which remains unswayed by the romantic love or the merry madness of this comedy world. Like him, she knows how to please her mistress with loyalty, and, as when Malvolio begins to act on the letter she has written in her mistress's hand, with pretended innocence which is very amusing:

He's coming, madam; but in very strange manner. He is sure possessed, madam. (III.iv.8–9)

She dislikes Malvolio, and both the tricks played on him – the letter which makes him appear mad and the interview with "Sir Topas" – are her ideas. When Malvolio reaches the lowest depth of unhappiness, Maria's work is done, and she leaves the stage and the play accompanied by Sir Toby. He comes back later wounded in the head and more than ever in need of her care. We understand from Fabian (V.i.345) that Sir Toby marries her, and we are hardly surprised. We may not be able to imagine them living happily ever after, as will Orsino with Viola and Olivia with Sebastian, but we know at least that their life together will never be dull.

Fabian is one of Olivia's trusted servants, but he, with the others, very much dislikes Malvolio. Fabian was in trouble with his mistress over the question of bear-baiting, and it was Malvolio who informed against him (II.v.6–7). This and

> some stubborn and uncourteous parts
> We have conceived against him (V.i.342–3)

encourage Fabian to take a leading part with Sir Toby in mocking Malvolio, although of the two Fabian is more cautious, calling for peace when he, Sir Toby, and Sir Andrew are watching Malvolio from behind the box-tree, and in the end admitting fully to his part in the deception. Because Olivia recognizes his frankness and honesty, she asks him to take over the reading of Malvolio's letter from Feste, whom she mistrusts (V.i.284).

Antonio gives his own account of his part in the play in V.i.68–83. He had saved Sebastian from drowning, and when the play begins he has come to like him so much that he decides to follow him and help him to find his way about town. But this puts Antonio in great danger, for he had fought against the Duke Orsino at sea, and had never made peace with him. Antonio gives Sebastian his purse for safe keeping, and, when he is arrested, asks it back from his twin, "Cesario", whom he has already saved from fighting a duel. Viola soon understands what has happened, and is able to save him from the Duke's anger.

DRAMATIS PERSONAE

ORSINO, *Duke of Illyria*

SEBASTIAN, *Viola's brother*

ANTONIO, *a Sea Captain, Sebastian's friend*

VALENTINE ⎫
CURIO ⎭ *gentlemen attending on the Duke*

SIR TOBY BELCH, *Olivia's uncle*

SIR ANDREW AGUECHEEK

MALVOLIO, *Olivia's steward*

FABIAN ⎫
FESTE, *the Clown* ⎭ *Olivia's servants*

A SEA CAPTAIN, *Viola's friend*

OLIVIA, *a rich Countess*

VIOLA, *in love with Orsino*

MARIA, *Olivia's woman*

LORDS, PRIESTS, SAILORS, OFFICERS, MUSICIANS AND
OTHER ATTENDANTS

———————

The scenes are laid in a city of Illyria and on the sea-coast near it.

(1.i) In this scene Orsino, the Duke of Illyria, tells of his love for the Countess Olivia, and hears that she has shut herself up in deep mourning for her dead brother.

1 *surfeiting, The appetite* – "the appetite, taking too much".

2 *That strain again!* – "Play that piece of music (*strain*) again!" He is talking to the musicians.

3 *a dying fall* – "an ending which died away".

4 *notwithstanding thy capacity . . . sea* – "although your capacity takes in as much as the sea itself".

5 *Of what validity . . . soe'er* – "whatever its value (*validity*) or degree of excellence (*pitch*) may be".

6 *falls into abatement* – "loses its value". The general sense of lines 9–13 is: "Spirit of love! how lively and quick to change you are! So much so that, although your capacity is as great as the sea itself, nothing, whatever its value, comes to you without losing its worth."

7 *so full of shapes . . . fantastical* – "love (*fancy*) is so full of images (*shapes*) that it is more imaginative (*fantastical*) than anything else (*alone*)".

8 *hart.* The duke plays on *hart* and *heart*; he calls his *heart: the noblest that I have,* i.e. "the noblest part of me", in the next line.

[handwritten: Duke characteristics — moody, sentimental, food of music]

ACT ONE

Scene I. A Room in the Duke's Palace.
Enter DUKE, CURIO, Lords; Musicians *attending.*

DUKE

If music be the food of love, play on;
Give me excess of it, that, surfeiting,
The appetite[1] may sicken, and so die.
That strain again![2] it had a dying fall;[3]
O, it came o'er my ear like the sweet sound   5
That breathes upon a bank of violets,
Stealing and giving odour. Enough! no more;
'T is not so sweet now as it was before.
O spirit of love! how quick and fresh art thou,
That, notwithstanding thy capacity   10
Receiveth as the sea,[4] nought enters there,
Of what validity and pitch soe'er,[5]
But falls into abatement[6] and low price,
Even in a minute; so full of shapes is fancy
That it alone is high fantastical.[7]   15

CURIO

Will you go hunt, my lord?

DUKE

What, Curio?

CURIO

The hart.[8]

DUKE

Why, so I do, the noblest that I have.
O, when mine eyes did see Olivia first,
Methought she purged the air of pestilence;

1

9 *That instant was I* (line 20) . . . *pursue me.* In a classical story Actaeon was turned into a hart by Diana, the goddess of hunting, because he looked at her while she was bathing. His own dogs then tore him to pieces.

10 *How now!* – "Well?" (as he sees Valentine entering).

11 *So please my lord* – "Please (hear the message), my lord".

12 *I might not be admitted* – "I was not allowed to go in". He has just returned from an unsuccessful journey to see Olivia.

13 *The element itself . . . heat* – "The very sky (*element*), for seven summers (*years' heat*)".

14 *behold* – "look on".

15 *ample* – "full".

16 *cloistress* – woman who devotes her life to religion in company with other women.

17 *water once a day . . . brine* – "weep bitter salt tears (*eye-offending brine*) once each day as she walks round her chamber".

18 *season* – "keep fresh", as the salt would do to food in the *brine* just mentioned.

19 *a heart . . . pay* – "a heart of such tender condition (*fine frame*) as to pay".

20 *the rich golden shaft.* People who fell in love were supposed to have been hit by the gold-tipped arrow (*shaft*) of Cupid, the god of love.

21 *all affections else* – "all other affections".

22 *liver, brain, and heart* (line 36) . . . *king!* Various parts of the body were thought to be the "seats" of different human qualities: passions in the liver, judgement in the brain, affections in the heart. From these "seats" or *thrones* (line 37) they ruled the body, and are therefore called *sovereign*, i.e. "ruling": "when these 'seats' which rule (various affections) the liver, the brain, the heart, are all supplied, and her sweet perfections fulfilled, by one king only (*self king*) (i.e. love – for me)".

23 *bowers* – "shelters of leafy branches".

*That instant was I turned into a hart
And my desires, like fell and cruel hounds,
E'er since pursue me*[9]

2

That instant was I turned into a hart,
And my desires, like fell and cruel hounds,
E'er since pursue me.[9]

Enter VALENTINE

[To VALENTINE]   How now![10] What news from her?

VALENTINE

So please my lord,[11] I might not be admitted;[12]
But from her handmaid do return this answer:
The element itself, till seven years' heat,[13]
Shall not behold[14] her face at ample[15] view;
But, like a cloistress,[16] she will veiléd walk,
And water once a day her chamber round
With eye-offending brine;[17] all this to season[18]
A brother's dead love, which she would keep fresh
And lasting in her sad remembrance.

DUKE

O, she that hath a heart of that fine frame
To pay[19] this debt of love but to a brother,
How will she love, when the rich golden shaft[20]
Hath killed the flock of all affections else[21]
That live in her; when liver, brain, and heart,
These sovereign thrones, are all supplied, and filled
Her sweet perfections, with one self king![22]
Away before me to sweet beds of flowers;
Love-thoughts lie rich when canopied with bowers.[23]

[Exeunt

Scene II. The Sea-coast.

Enter VIOLA, Captain, and Sailors.

VIOLA

What country, friends, is this?

3

(I.ii) Viola and the Captain have just escaped drowning in a shipwreck off the coast of Illyria; it seems possible that Sebastian, Viola's twin brother, who was with her on board, also escaped from the wreck, but she fears that he is drowned. The Captain tells her about Orsino, and she decides to disguise herself and go to court to serve him.

1 *Illyria* was the name given in Shakespeare's day to a land lying on the eastern side of the Adriatic Sea.

2 In classical times, the souls of those who died blessed were thought to go to a part of the lower world called *Elysium*. The name *Illyria* reminds Viola of *Elysium*, a home of the dead to which her brother, she fears, has gone.

3 *perchance* – "by good luck". Viola uses this word in the line before, but in its ordinary sense, "perhaps", and the Captain takes it up.

4 *to comfort you with chance* – "so that you may take comfort from what is possible".

5 *those poor number* – "those few people", perhaps the sailors who are standing near by.

6 *driving* – "moved only by the wind and waves".

7 *the practice* – "how to do it".

8 *lived* – "floated".

9 *Arion on the dolphin's back*. Arion was, according to a classical story, a Greek musician. Once, in a treasure-ship, the seamen planned to murder him, but he jumped into the sea and a dolphin, charmed by his music, carried him away on its back.

10 *hold acquaintance* – "keep company". He did not sink below the waves.

11 *Mine own escape (line 17) . . . like of him* – "my own escape gives me hope (and what you have told me (*thy speech*) serves to support it) that he has escaped too". (*The like of him* – i.e. "the same has happened to him".)

CAPTAIN

This is Illyria,[1] lady.

VIOLA

And what should I do in Illyria?
My brother he is in Elysium.[2] *Heaven*
Perchance he is not drowned; what think you, sailors?

CAPTAIN

It is perchance[3] that you yourself were saved.   5

VIOLA

O, my poor brother! and so perchance may he be.

CAPTAIN

True, madam; and, to comfort you with chance,[4]
Assure yourself, after our ship did split,
When you and those poor number[5] saved with you
Hung on our driving[6] boat, I saw your brother,   10
Most provident in peril, bind himself –
Courage and hope both teaching him the practice[7] –
To a strong mast that lived[8] upon the sea;
Where, like Arion on the dolphin's back,[9] *greek poet + musician*
I saw him hold acquaintance[10] with the waves   15
So long as I could see.

VIOLA

[*Giving him money*]   For saying so, there's gold;
Mine own escape unfoldeth to my hope,
Whereto thy speech serves for authority,
The like of him.[11] Know'st thou this country?

CAPTAIN

Ay, madam, well; for I was bred and born   20
Not three hours' travel from this very place.

12 *A noble duke . . . in name*; he was as
noble in his character (*nature*) as he
was in his birth.

13 *late* – "recently".

14 *fresh in murmur* – "just being talked
about".

15 *the less* – "less important people".

VIOLA

Who governs here?

CAPTAIN

A noble duke, in nature as in name.[12]

VIOLA

What is his name?

CAPTAIN

Orsino.   25

VIOLA

Orsino! I have heard my father name him;
He was a bachelor then.

CAPTAIN

And so is now, or was so very late;[13]
For but a month ago I went from hence,
And then 't was fresh in murmur[14] – as, you know,   30
What great ones do the less[15] will prattle of –
That he did seek the love of fair Olivia.

VIOLA

What 's she?

CAPTAIN

A virtuous maid, the daughter of a count
That died some twelvemonth since; then leaving her   35
In the protection of his son, her brother,
Who shortly also died; for whose dear love,
They say, she hath abjured the company
And sight of men.

16 *delivered* – "made known".

17 *Till I had made . . . estate is* – "until I had made a good (*mellow*) opportunity (for declaring) who I am (*what my estate is*)". She wants to conceal her origin until she sees her way clear to going back home.

18 *That were hard to compass* – "That would be difficult to bring about".

19 *There is a fair behaviour in thee* – "You have a pleasant look and manner".

20 *though that nature . . . pollution* – "although (*though that*) nature often surrounds foulness (*pollution*) with a beautiful enclosure (*beauteous wall*)"; what is beautiful outside is not necessarily beautiful inside.

21 *suits With* – "matches".

22 *haply shall become . . . my intent* – "perhaps (*haply*) shall suit the nature of my purpose". The disguise is to be the dress of a page.

23 *pains* – "trouble".

24 *That will allow . . . service* – "that will prove (*allow*) me to be very worthy of serving him".

25 *hap* – "happen".

26 *mute* – "silent watcher". The *eunuch* was usually dumb.

8

VIOLA

O that I served that lady,
And might not be delivered[16] to the world   40
Till I had made mine own occasion mellow,
What my estate is![17]

CAPTAIN

That were hard to compass,[18]
Because she will admit no kind of suit,
No, not the duke's.

VIOLA

There is a fair behaviour in thee,[19] captain;   45
And though that nature with a beauteous wall
Doth oft close in pollution,[20] yet of thee
I will believe thou hast a mind that suits
With[21] this thy fair and outward character.
I prithee – and I 'll pay thee bounteously –   50
Conceal me what I am, and be my aid
For such disguise as haply shall become
The form of my intent.[22] I 'll serve this duke;
Thou shalt present me as an eunuch to him;
It may be worth thy pains;[23] for I can sing   55
And speak to him in many sorts of music
That will allow me very worth his service.[24]
What else may hap,[25] to time I will commit;
Only shape thou thy silence to my wit.

CAPTAIN

Be you his eunuch, and your mute[26] I 'll be;   60
When my tongue blabs, then let mine eyes not see.

VIOLA

I thank thee; lead me on.

[*Exeunt*

9

(I.iii) Maria complains to Sir Toby of his bad behaviour in Olivia's house. She also speaks about the foolishness of Sir Andrew, who is said to have come to woo Olivia. Then Sir Andrew himself appears; he boasts of his accomplishments, but fears that he may never be able to win Olivia's hand in marriage.

1 *What a plague ... to take ... –* "What the devil does my niece mean by taking ...".
2 *By my troth –* "Indeed".
3 *o' nights –* "at night".
4 *takes great exceptions ... hours –* "objects very strongly to your irregular habits (*ill hours*)".

5 *let her except before excepted –* "let her object to what has been objected to before". Sir Toby uses a legal phrase to make fun of Maria's last words, but it makes no sense here.
6 *I'll confine myself ... I am –* "I'll dress myself no more finely than I am now". Again Sir Toby makes fun of Maria's words; he purposely misunderstands her, and then uses *finer* to further the change of meaning.

Scene III. A Room in Olivia's House.
Enter SIR TOBY BELCH and MARIA.

SIR TOBY

What a plague means my niece, to take[1] the death of her
brother thus? I am sure care's an enemy to life.

MARIA

By my troth,[2] Sir Toby, you must come in earlier o' nights;[3]
your cousin, my lady, takes great exceptions to your ill hours.[4]

SIR TOBY

Why, let her except before excepted.[5]   5

MARIA

Ay, but you must confine yourself within the modest limits
of order.

SIR TOBY

Confine! I'll confine myself no finer than I am.[6] These clothes
are good enough to drink in, and so be these boots too; an they
be not, let them hang themselves in their own straps.   10

MARIA

That quaffing and drinking will undo you; I heard my lady talk
of it yesterday; and of a foolish knight that you brought in one
night here to be her wooer.

SIR TOBY

Who? Sir Andrew Aguecheek?

MARIA

Ay, he.   15

11

7 *tall* – "brave".

8 *he has three thousand ducats* – "he has an income of three thousand ducats". A ducat was a gold or silver coin worth about one-third of a pound sterling.

9 *but he'll have ... ducats* – "but he will use up all these ducats in one year".

10 *the viol-de-gamboys* – an old type of large stringed musical instrument.

11 *without book* – "by heart".

12 *almost natural* – "almost like a born fool (*natural*)"; but Maria can be taken to mean also: "all, most natural(ly)".

13 *allay the gust* – "quieten the delight".

14 *substractors*. This is Sir Toby's mistake for *detractors*. Thinking it sounds like *subtract*, Maria talks of *adding* in the next line.

15 *coystril* – "a low fellow".

16 *a parish-top*. A large top, made to spin quickly by beating it with whips, was once kept in many villages. In cold weather men used to whip it to keep themselves occupied and warm while they could not work.

17 *Castiliano vulgo*. Although "Castilian" was used in a number of exclamations in Shakespeare's day, this phrase of Sir Toby's has not been explained. It is most probably meaningless, but fine and foreign-sounding so as to impress Maria.

He plays o' the viol-de-gamboys[10]

SIR TOBY

He 's as tall[7] a man as any 's in Illyria.

MARIA

What 's that to the purpose?

SIR TOBY

Why, he has three thousand ducats[8] a year.

MARIA

Ay, but he 'll have but a year in all these ducats;[9] he 's a very
fool and a prodigal.   20

SIR TOBY

Fie, that you 'll say so! He plays o' the viol-de-gamboys,[10] and
speaks three or four languages word for word without book,[11]
and hath all the good gifts of nature.

MARIA

He hath indeed, almost natural;[12] for besides that he 's a fool,
he 's a great quarreller; and but that he hath the gift of a coward   25
to allay the gust[13] he hath in quarrelling, 't is thought among the
prudent he would quickly have the gift of a grave.

SIR TOBY

By this hand, they are scoundrels and substractors[14] that say so
of him. Who are they?

MARIA

They that add, moreover, he 's drunk nightly in your company.   30

SIR TOBY

With drinking healths to my niece. I 'll drink to her as long as
there is a passage in my throat and drink in Illyria. He 's a coward
and a coystril[15] that will not drink to my niece till his brains turn
o' the toe like a parish-top.[16] What, wench! *Castiliano vulgo!*[17]
for here comes Sir Andrew Agueface.   35

13

18 *shrew* – "a disagreeable woman";
but Sir Andrew, not knowing what
the word means, uses it as if it were
a compliment.

19 *Accost* – "Greet (her)". But Sir
Andrew does not know the word,
and asks *What's that?* – "What does
that mean?" (line 41). Sir Toby
misunderstands him, or pretends to,
and tells him what sort of a person
Maria is (line 42). Then Sir Andrew
assumes that her name is Accost
(line 43).

14

Enter SIR ANDREW AGUECHEEK

SIR ANDREW

Sir Toby Belch! How now, Sir Toby Belch!

SIR TOBY

Sweet Sir Andrew!

SIR ANDREW

[*To* MARIA] Bless you, fair shrew.[18]

MARIA

And you too, sir.

SIR TOBY

Accost,[19] Sir Andrew, accost.   40

SIR ANDREW

What 's that?

SIR TOBY

My niece's chambermaid.

SIR ANDREW

Good Mistress Accost, I desire better acquaintance.

MARIA

My name is Mary, sir.

SIR ANDREW

Good Mistress Mary Accost –   45

SIR TOBY

You mistake, knight; "accost" is front her, board her, woo her, assail her.

15

20 *Fare you well* – "Good-bye".

21 *An thou let part so* – "If you let her go away like this".

22 *you have fools in hand* – "you are dealing with fools".

23 *I have not you by the hand*. Maria makes a joke on Sir Andrew's phrase *in hand*, "dealing with"; "I am not holding *you* by the hand (so there is at least *one* fool I am not dealing with)".

24 *bring your hand . . . drink*. This was a saying used to ask for a kiss and a present. The *buttery-bar* was a shelf above the low doorway through which food and drink were served out from a store.

25 *your metaphor* – "the real meaning of what you have just said".

26 *It 's dry*, i.e. "your hand is dry". This suggests that he lacks passion; and when he says in the next line, *I am not such an ass but I can keep my hand dry*, he means he does not fall passionately in love with every girl he meets.

SIR ANDREW

By my troth, I would not undertake her in this company. Is that the meaning of "accost"?

MARIA

Fare you well,[20] gentlemen.   50

SIR TOBY

An thou let part so,[21] Sir Andrew, would thou might'st never draw sword again!

SIR ANDREW

An you part so, mistress, I would I might never draw sword again. Fair lady, do you think you have fools in hand?[22]

MARIA

Sir, I have not you by the hand.[23]   55

SIR ANDREW

Marry, but you shall have; and here's my hand.

MARIA

Now, sir, "thought is free"; I pray you, bring your hand to the buttery-bar and let it drink.[24]

SIR ANDREW

Wherefore, sweetheart? What's your metaphor?[25]

MARIA

It's dry,[26] sir.   60

SIR ANDREW

Why, I think so; I am not such an ass but I can keep my hand dry. But what's your jest?

27 *A dry jest* – "A silly joke". The word *dry* is now being used for something else.

28 *at my fingers' ends* – "always ready"; and, literally, "at the ends of her fingers", where she has hold of Sir Andrew, who is himself *dry*, "silly".

29 *barren* – "unable to make any more jokes".

30 *thou lackest a cup of canary* – "you need a cup of canary wine (to make you feel happier)".

31 *so put down* – "made to look so foolish".

32 *wit* – "intelligence", particularly that by which people are able to make good, humorous conversation.

33 *forswear it* – "give it up; not eat it any more".

34 *Pourquoi* (French) – "Why". But Sir Andrew does not understand.

35 *in the tongues* – "in the study of foreign languages". In Shakespeare's day, *tongue* and *tong* seem to have been pronounced alike. In line 80 Sir Toby jokes on *tongues*, taking the word to mean curling-tongs for the hair. If Sir Andrew had spent much time with the *tongs*, he would have had a fine head of hair.

18

MARIA

A dry jest,[27] sir.

SIR ANDREW

Are you full of them?

MARIA

Ay, sir, I have them at my fingers' ends;[28] marry, now I let go 65
your hand, I am barren.[29]

                                                          [*Exit*

SIR TOBY

O knight! thou lackest a cup of canary;[30] when did I see thee so
put down?[31]

SIR ANDREW

Never in your life, I think; unless you see canary put me down.
Methinks sometimes I have no more wit[32] than a Christian or an 70
ordinary man has; but I am a great eater of beef, and I believe
that does harm to my wit.

SIR TOBY

No question.

SIR ANDREW

An I thought that, I 'd forswear it.[33] I 'll ride home tomorrow,
Sir Toby.   75

SIR TOBY

Pourquoi,[34] my dear knight?

SIR ANDREW

What is "*pourquoi*"? Do or not do? I would I had bestowed that
time in the tongues[35] that I have in fencing, dancing, and bear-
baiting. O! had I but followed the arts!

36 *mended* – "improved".

37 *your niece will not be seen* – "I cannot get to see your niece (Olivia)".

38 *she 'll none of me* – "she will have nothing to do with me". (The phrase is used again in line 89 below.)

39 *here hard by* – "(who lives) very near here".

40 *she 'll not match . . . nor wit* – "she will not marry (*match*) above her own social position, either in fortune, age, or intelligence".

41 *Tut, there 's . . . man* – "Nonsense, the case is not hopeless, man".

42 *kickshawses* – "trifles".

it hangs like flax on a distaff

20

SIR TOBY

Then hadst thou had an excellent head of hair.   80

SIR ANDREW

Why, would that have mended[36] my hair?

SIR TOBY

Past question; for thou seest it will not curl by nature.

SIR ANDREW

But it becomes me well enough, does it not?

SIR TOBY

Excellent; it hangs like flax on a distaff, and I hope to see a
housewife take thee between her legs, and spin it off.   85

SIR ANDREW

Faith, I 'll home tomorrow, Sir Toby; your niece will not be
seen;[37] or if she be, it 's four to one she 'll none of me.[38] The
count himself here hard by[39] woos her.

SIR TOBY

She 'll none o' the count; she 'll not match above her degree,
neither in estate, years, nor wit;[40] I have heard her swear it. Tut,   90
there 's life in 't, man.[41]

SIR ANDREW

I 'll stay a month longer. I am a fellow o' the strangest mind i'
the world; I delight in masques and revels sometimes altogether.

SIR TOBY

Art thou good at these kickshawses,[42] knight?   95

21

43 *As any man in Illyria . . . old man.*
Sir Andrew says, in effect, that he
is as good at these things as anyone who is not better than he is. He
will not compare with his *betters*,
nor with a practised (*old*) man.

44 *cut a caper* – "dance a good step".
But Sir Toby purposely misunderstands, and takes him to mean that
he can cut slices of *capers* (a kind of
pickle); Sir Toby says he can cut
the meat (*the mutton*) to go with it.

45 *I have the back-trick* – "I can do the
step backwards" (in dancing).

46 *are they like . . . picture?* – "are they
likely to be damaged by dust, like
Mistress Mall's picture?" It was
the custom to protect particularly
valuable pictures by hanging a curtain in front of them. It is not
known who Mistress Mall was.

47 *coranto* – a lively dance.

48 *sink-a-pace* – a dance with a five-
beat rhythm.

49 *under the star of a galliard.* Men's
characters and skills were supposed
to be formed by the influence of the
stars and particularly by their positions in the sky at the time of birth.
Sir Toby suggests that being born
"under" a certain star gave one skill
in dancing.

50 *does indifferent well* – "looks rather
well".

51 *flame-coloured stock* – "bright yellow
stocking".

SIR ANDREW

As any man in Illyria, whatsoever he be, under the degree of my
betters; and yet I will not compare with an old man.[43]

SIR TOBY

What is thy excellence in a galliard, knight?

SIR ANDREW

Faith, I can cut a caper.[44]

SIR TOBY

And I can cut the mutton to 't.   100

SIR ANDREW

And I think I have the back-trick[45] simply as strong as any man
in Illyria.   [*He dances*

SIR TOBY

Wherefore are these things hid? Wherefore have these gifts a
curtain before 'em? Are they like to take dust, like Mistress
Mall's picture?[46] Why dost thou not go to church in a galliard,   105
and come home in a coranto?[47] My very walk should be a jig;
I would not so much as make water but in a sink-a-pace.[48] What
dost thou mean? Is it a world to hide virtues in? I did think, by
the excellent constitution of thy leg, it was formed under the
star of a galliard.[49]   110

SIR ANDREW

Ay, 't is strong, and it does indifferent well[50] in a flame-coloured
stock.[51] Shall we set about some revels?

SIR TOBY

What shall we do else? Were we not born under Taurus?

52 *Taurus! that 's sides and heart.* They are again referring to the influence of the heavenly bodies at a person's birth. Taurus (the Bull) is a sign of the Zodiac. Each sign was said to control a particular part of the body and the affection supposedly seated in it, though in fact Taurus was associated with the neck and throat, not the sides and heart.

(I.iv) Viola has now taken service as a page in the Duke's palace, and she is already much in favour there. The Duke has told her of his love for Olivia, and sends her to woo his lady for him.

1 VIOLA *in man's attire.* Viola appears in man's dress, talking to one of the Duke's gentlemen, and later in the scene much play is made of the fact that the audience knows she is a woman but the Duke does not.

2 *like* – "likely".

3 *his humour* – "his temperament", i.e. that he is uncertain in temper, changeable.

4 *Who saw Cesario, ho?* – "Has anyone seen Cesario?"

5 *On your attendance* – "(I am waiting) at your service".

in man's attire[1]

24

SIR ANDREW

Taurus! that 's sides and heart.[52]

SIR TOBY

No, sir, it is legs and thighs. Let me see thee caper. [SIR ANDREW 115 *dances again*] Ha! higher; ha, ha! excellent!

[*Exeunt*

Scene IV. A Room in the Duke's Palace.
Enter VALENTINE, *and* VIOLA *in man's attire.*[1]

VALENTINE

If the duke continue these favours towards you, Cesario, you are like[2] to be much advanced; he hath known you but three days and already you are no stranger.

VIOLA [*who has taken the name* CESARIO]

You either fear his humour[3] or my negligence, that you call in question the continuance of his love. Is he inconstant, sir, in his   5 favours?

VALENTINE

No, believe me.

VIOLA

I thank you. Here comes the count.

Enter DUKE, CURIO, *and* Attendants

DUKE

Who saw Cesario, ho?[4]

VIOLA

On your attendance,[5] my lord; here.   10

25

6 *but* – "than".

7 *I have unclasped . . . secret soul.* The Duke has told Viola even his deepest secrets, and speaks of them as a book which is kept closed with a *clasp* (see Glossary). They concern his love for Olivia.

8 *address thy gait* – "make your way".

9 *Till thou have audience* – "until you are allowed to see and speak (to Olivia)".

10 *As it is spoke* – "as people say".

11 *leap all civil bounds* – "jump over, go beyond, all limits of good manners".

12 *dear* – "heartfelt".

13 *attend it* – "take notice of it".

14 *a nuncio's of more grave aspect* – "a messenger (*nuncio*) of more serious appearance (*aspect*)". Strictly, Viola's youth is contrasted with the youth of the *nuncio*; but the Duke evidently refers to an older messenger.

15 *they shall yet . . . a man* – "those people (*they*) who say you are a man mistake your age (*belie thy . . . years*)". To the Duke "Cesario" seems still a boy.

26

DUKE

[*To the* Attendants] Stand you awhile aloof. [*To* VIOLA] Cesario,
Thou know'st no less but[6] all; I have unclasped
To thee the book even of my secret soul.[7]
Therefore, good youth, address thy gait[8] unto her;
Be not denied access, stand at her doors,   15
And tell them, there thy fixéd foot shall grow
Till thou have audience.[9]

VIOLA

          Sure, my noble lord,
If she be so abandoned to her sorrow
As it is spoke,[10] she never will admit me.

DUKE

Be clamorous, and leap all civil bounds,[11]   20
Rather than make unprofited return.

VIOLA

Say I do speak with her, my lord; what then?

DUKE

O! then unfold the passion of my love;
Surprise her with discourse of my dear[12] faith;
It shall become thee well to act my woes;   25
She will attend it[13] better in thy youth
Than in a nuncio's of more grave aspect.[14]

VIOLA

I think not so, my lord.

DUKE

          Dear lad, believe it;
For they shall yet belie thy happy years
That say thou art a man;[15] Diana's lip   30

16 *Diana's lip . . . rubious* – "the lips of Diana (the beautiful goddess of hunting and of the moon) are not more smooth and red (than yours)".

17 *thy small pipe* – "your high-pitched voice".

18 *all is semblative a woman's part* – "everything (about you) resembles a woman's character". There is probably also a reference here to the fact that in Shakespeare's day boys played the parts of women on the stage.

19 *constellation* – "character", as influenced by the stars. (See note 49 to I.iii.)

20 *a barful strife* – "a struggle full of difficulties".

21 *myself would be his wife* – "I myself would like to be his wife".

(I.v) Feste, Olivia's clown, has been away without leave, and fears his mistress's anger. He does his best to amuse her when she comes in with Malvolio her steward, but Malvolio is too serious to enjoy clowning. Viola, disguised as a boy and calling herself "Cesario", arrives from Orsino, and refuses to allow herself to be turned away, so that at last she is brought before Olivia, who veils herself. Viola begins her prepared speech, but she and Olivia soon start to talk freely, and when "Cesario" leaves, Olivia quickly recognizes that she has fallen in love with "him". Pretending that Viola has forced her to accept a ring from Orsino, she sends Malvolio after Viola with a ring of her own, and a message asking her to come again.

1 *in way of thy excuse* – "to make excuses for you". He has perhaps been at Orsino's house, and Maria fears that Olivia will want to know why.

2 *to fear no colours* – "have no fears". The *colours* were originally the flags of the enemy in war, as Maria goes on to explain, but the phrase was a common one, and Feste used it because *colours* sounds like *collars*, a word suggested by the talk of hanging.

3 *Make that good* – "Prove what you say".

Is not more smooth and rubious;[16] thy small pipe[17]
Is as the maiden's organ, shrill and sound,
And all is semblative a woman's part.[18]
I know thy constellation[19] is right apt
For this affair. [To the Attendants] Some four or five attend   35
   him –
All, if you will; for I myself am best
When least in company. Prosper well in this,
And thou shalt live as freely as thy lord,
To call his fortune thine.

VIOLA

       I 'll do my best
To woo your lady. [Aside] Yet, a barful strife![20]
Whoe'er I woo, myself would be his wife.[21]   40

[Exeunt

Scene V. A Room in Olivia's House.

Enter MARIA and FESTE, the clown.

MARIA

Nay, either tell me where thou hast been, or I will not open my
lips so wide as a bristle may enter in way of thy excuse.[1] My
lady will hang thee for thy absence.

FESTE

Let her hang me; he that is well hanged in this world needs to
fear no colours.[2]   5

MARIA

Make that good.[3]

FESTE

He shall see none to fear.

29

4 *lenten* – "plain".

5 *that may you . . . foolery* – "you can at least be bold enough to say *that* when you are playing the fool".

6 *Well, God give . . . their talents.* This sounds nonsense, and is probably a purposely falsified form of some saying. It is possibly an echo of the phrase used in the Bible story of the talents: *For unto every one that hath shall be given* (Matthew xxv. 29).

7 *to be turned away* – "dismissed from your post".

8 *for turning away . . . it out* – "as for being dismissed, the summer makes it bearable". (The action of the play takes place in summertime.)

9 *two points* – "two matters"; but Maria uses *points* to mean "laces holding up trousers".

10 *gaskins* – "trousers".

11 *if Sir Toby would (line 22) . . . in Illyria.* He is suggesting that Maria and Sir Toby might get married; "if Sir Toby would give up drinking, you would be as attractive a woman (for him to marry) as any in Illyria".

MARIA

A good lenten[4] answer; I can tell thee where that saying was born, of "I fear no colours".

FESTE

Where, good Mistress Mary?   10

MARIA

In the wars; and that may you be bold to say in your foolery.[5]

FESTE

Well, God give them wisdom that have it; and those that are fools, let them use their talents.[6]

MARIA

Yet you will be hanged for being so long absent; or, to be turned away,[7] is not that as good as a hanging to you?   15

FESTE

Many a good hanging prevents a bad marriage; and, for turning away, let summer bear it out.[8]

MARIA

You are resolute, then?

FESTE

Not so, neither; but I am resolved on two points.[9]

MARIA

That if one break, the other will hold; or, if both break, your   20 gaskins[10] fall.

FESTE

Apt, in good faith; very apt. Well, go thy way; if Sir Toby would leave drinking, thou wert as witty a piece of Eve's flesh as any in Illyria.[11]

31

12 *you were best* – "it will be best for you".

13 *Wit.* The Clown prays that Wit may come to him in his need; for his lady may be angry with him, and only quick, clever answers will appease her.

14 *thee*, i.e. Wit.

15 *Quinapalus.* The Clown makes up the name of a writer, and pretends that he wrote this saying.

16 *Go to* – "Don't talk nonsense".

17 *dry* – "dull".

18 *I 'll no more of you* – "I 'll have nothing more to do with you".

19 *madonna* – "my lady".

20 *mend* – "improve". The word is frequently used with the same meaning in this scene.

21 *botcher* – "one who mends clothes unskilfully".

22 *As there is no . . . a flower.* The Clown's reasoning has suggested that no man or woman is all good or all bad; they are *patched*. *Cuckold* must be his mistake for a word such as "counsellor": "calamity is the only worthwhile counsellor"; and "beauty is like a flower", which will fade in time.

MARIA

Peace, you rogue, no more o' that. Here comes my lady; make   25
your excuse wisely, you were best.[12]

[*Exit*

FESTE

Wit,[13] an 't be thy will, put me into good fooling! Those wits
that think they have thee,[14] do very oft prove fools; and I, that
am sure I lack thee, may pass for a wise man; for what says
Quinapalus?[15] "Better a witty fool than a foolish wit."   30

Enter OLIVIA, MALVOLIO, *and* Attendants

God bless thee, lady!

OLIVIA

Take the fool away.

FESTE

[*To the* Attendants] Do you not hear, fellows? Take away the
lady.

OLIVIA

[*To* FESTE] Go to,[16] you 're a dry[17] fool; I 'll no more of you;[18]   35
besides, you grow dishonest.

FESTE

Two faults, madonna,[19] that drink and good counsel will amend;
for give the dry fool drink, then is the fool not dry; bid the dishonest man mend[20] himself; if he mend, he is no longer dishonest; if he cannot, let the botcher[21] mend him. Anything   40
that 's mended is but patched; virtue that transgresses is but
patched with sin; and sin that amends is but patched with virtue. If that this simple syllogism will serve, so; if it will not,
what remedy? As there is no true cuckold but calamity, so
beauty 's a flower.[22] The lady bade take away the fool; there-   45
fore, I say again, take her away.

23 *Misprision* means both "mistake" and "scorn".
24 *cucullus non facit monachum* (Latin) – "a hood does not make a monk", a proverb meaning, "you cannot always tell what people are like by the clothes they wear".
25 *I wear not ... brain* – "I wear the dress of a court fool (*motley*) on my body but not in my brain", i.e. "my clothes do not make me a fool".
26 *Dexteriously* is an unusual form of *dexterously*, used by the Clown perhaps in fun.
27 *good my mouse of virtue* – "my good, virtuous little woman".
28 *for want of other idleness* – "since I have no other pastime".
29 *I'll bide your proof* – "I'll wait while you are proving (what you just said)".

I wear not motley in my brain[25]

34

OLIVIA

Sir, I bade them take away *you*.

FESTE

Misprision[23] in the highest degree! Lady, *cucullus non facit mona-chum*:[24] that's as much to say as I wear not motley in my brain.[25] Good madonna, give me leave to prove you a fool.　　　　50

OLIVIA

Can you do it?

FESTE

Dexteriously,[26] good madonna.

OLIVIA

Make your proof.

FESTE

I must catechize you for it, madonna; good my mouse of virtue,[27] answer me.　　　　55

OLIVIA

Well, sir, for want of other idleness,[28] I'll bide your proof.[29]

FESTE

Good madonna, why mournest thou?

OLIVIA

Good fool, for my brother's death.

FESTE

I think his soul is in hell, madonna.

OLIVIA

I know his soul is in heaven, fool.　　　　60

30 *pass his word* – "pledge his word".
31 *barren* – "empty (of brains), foolish".
32 *put down . . . with* – "beaten in a battle of wit . . . by".
33 *out of his guard* – "not prepared to defend himself".
34 *minister occasion* – "give him opportunities (i.e. subjects) on which he can make jokes".
35 *I protest* – "I give it as my opinion".
36 *crow* – "laugh noisily".
37 *take (line 76) . . . no better* – "value . . . no more highly".

38 *free disposition* – "kind in character".
39 *bird-bolts* – short arrows for shooting down birds.
40 *allowed* – "licensed" by his master or mistress, and therefore able to make jokes at their expense; this, as Olivia says, cannot be called slander.
41 *though* – "even though".
42 *nor no* – "neither is there".
43 *a known discreet man* – "a man of recognized discretion".

the fools' zanies.

36

FESTE

The more fool, madonna, to mourn for your brother's soul being in heaven. [*To the* Attendants] Take away the fool, gentlemen.

OLIVIA

[*To* MALVOLIO] What think you of this fool, Malvolio? Doth he not mend? 65

MALVOLIO

Yes; and shall do till the pangs of death shake him; infirmity, that decays the wise, doth ever make the better fool.

FESTE

God send you, sir, a speedy infirmity, for the better increasing your folly! Sir Toby will be sworn that I am no fox, but he will not pass his word[30] for two pence that you are no fool. 70

OLIVIA

How say you to that, Malvolio?

MALVOLIO

I marvel your ladyship takes delight in such a barren[31] rascal; I saw him put down the other day with[32] an ordinary fool that has no more brain than a stone. Look you now, he's out of his guard[33] already; unless you laugh and minister occasion[34] to 75 him, he is gagged. I protest,[35] I take these wise men, that crow[36] so at these set kind of fools, no better[37] than the fools' zanies.

OLIVIA

O, you are sick of self-love, Malvolio, and taste with a distempered appetite. To be generous, guiltless, and of free disposition,[38] is to take those things for bird-bolts[39] that you deem 80 cannon-bullets. There is no slander in an allowed[40] fool, though[41] he do nothing but rail; nor no[42] railing in a known discreet man,[43] though he do nothing but reprove.

37

44 *Mercury endue thee with leasing.*
Mercury was said to be the god of
liars. "May Mercury give (*endue
... with*) you the gift of lying
(*leasing*)." He suggests there is
nothing good to say about court
fools if she is to talk about them
truthfully.

45 *much desires* – "who very much
wishes".

46 *hold him in delay* – "keep him
waiting".

47 *he speaks nothing but madman* – "he
speaks just like a madman".

48 *us*, i.e. court fools in general.

49 *Jove* – Jupiter, the king of the gods.

50 *one of thy kin has* – "one of your
kinsmen who has".

51 *pia mater* (Latin) – "brain" (more
correctly the soft skin which
covers the brain).

FESTE

Now, Mercury endue thee with leasing,[44] for thou speakest
well of fools!   85

Re-enter MARIA

MARIA

Madam, there is at the gate a young gentleman much desires[45]
to speak with you.

OLIVIA

From the count Orsino, is it?

MARIA

I know not, madam; 't is a fair young man, and well attended.

OLIVIA

Who of my people hold him in delay?[46]   90

MARIA

Sir Toby, madam, your kinsman.

OLIVIA

Fetch him off, I pray you; he speaks nothing but madman.[47] Fie
on him!   [*Exit* MARIA
Go you, Malvolio; if it be a suit from the count, I am sick, or
not at home, what you will, to dismiss it.   [*Exit* MALVOLIO]   95
[*To* FESTE] Now you see, sir, how your fooling grows old, and
people dislike it.

FESTE

Thou hast spoke for us,[48] madonna, as if thy eldest son should
be a fool; whose skull Jove[49] cram with brains! for here he
comes, one of thy kin has[50] a most weak *pia mater*.[51]   100

39

52 *What* – "What sort of a person".

53 *pickle-herring* were fish eaten with strong drink to give thirst. Sir Toby pretends that the disturbance in his stomach is caused not by the drink but by the pickled herrings, and curses them.

54 *Lechery*. He has misheard or mis-understood Olivia's word *lethargy*.

55 *one* – "someone".

56 *it 's all one* – "it 's all the same (to me)".

40

Enter SIR TOBY BELCH

OLIVIA

By mine honour, half drunk. [*To* SIR TOBY] What[52] is he at the
gate, cousin?

SIR TOBY

A gentleman.

OLIVIA

A gentleman! What gentleman?

SIR TOBY

'T is a gentleman here – a plague o' these pickle-herring![53] [*To* 105
FESTE] How now, sot!

FESTE

Good Sir Toby!

OLIVIA

Cousin, cousin, how have you come so early by this lethargy?

SIR TOBY

Lechery![54] I defy lechery. There 's one[55] at the gate.

OLIVIA

Ay, marry; what is he?   110

SIR TOBY

Let him be the devil, an he will, I care not; give me faith, say I.
Well, it 's all one.[56]

[*Exit*

OLIVIA

What 's a drunken man like, fool?

41

57 *above heat* – "more than he needs to quench his thirst".

58 *mads him* – "makes him mad".

59 *crowner* – "coroner".

60 *sit o' my coz* – "sit (in court) on the case of my kinsman", who may be taken as drowned with drink.

61 *Has* – "He has".

62 *sheriff's post*, such as was put up outside a sheriff's house to show his authority.

63 *be the supporter to a bench* – "hold up a bench".

64 *but . . .* In Modern English this part of the sentence would begin (line 129): "and he says he'll speak with you even if he stands at your door . . ."

SCENE V]

FESTE

Like a drowned man, a fool, and a madman; one draught above
heat[57] makes him a fool, the second mads him,[58] and a third 115
drowns him.

OLIVIA

Go thou and seek the crowner,[59] and let him sit o' my coz;[60] for
he 's in the third degree of drink, he 's drowned; go, look after
him.

FESTE

He is but mad yet, madonna; and the fool shall look to the 120
madman.

[*Exit*

Re-enter MALVOLIO

MALVOLIO

Madam, yond young fellow swears he will speak with you. I
told him you were sick; he takes on him to understand so much,
and therefore comes to speak with you. I told him you were
asleep; he seems to have a foreknowledge of that too, and there- 125
fore comes to speak with you. What is to be said to him, lady?
He 's fortified against any denial.

OLIVIA

Tell him he shall not speak with me.

MALVOLIO

Has[61] been told so; and he says he 'll stand at your door like a
sheriff's post,[62] and be the supporter to a bench,[63] but[64] he 'll 130
speak with you.

OLIVIA

What kind o' man is he?

43

65 *manner* – "kind".
66 *ill* – "bad".
67 *will you or no* – "whether you wish or not".
68 *a squash . . . a peascod* – "a pea-pod (*peascod*) before it is ripe"; *squash* – "an unripe pea-pod".
69 *codling* – "unripe apple".

70 *in standing water* – "like the sea at the changing of the tide", neither ebbing nor flowing but between them.
71 *well-favoured* – "handsome".
72 *shrewishly* – "sharply".
73 *embassy* – "message".

44

MALVOLIO

Why, of mankind.

OLIVIA

What manner[65] of man?

MALVOLIO

Of very ill[66] manner; he 'll speak with you, will you or no.[67]   135

OLIVIA

Of what personage and years is he?

MALVOLIO

Not yet old enough for a man, nor young enough for a boy; as
a squash is before 't is a peascod,[68] or a codling[69] when 't is
almost an apple; 't is with him in standing water,[70] between boy
and man. He is very well-favoured,[71] and he speaks very shrew-   140
ishly;[72] one would think his mother's milk were scarce out of
him.

OLIVIA

Let him approach. Call in my gentlewoman.

MALVOLIO

Gentlewoman, my lady calls.

[*Exit*

Re-enter MARIA

OLIVIA

Give me my veil; come, throw it o'er my face. We 'll once   145
more hear Orsino's embassy.[73]

Enter VIOLA *and* Attendants

VIOLA

The honourable lady of the house, which is she?

45

74 *Your will?* – "What do you want?"
Viola then begins the prepared
speech, but breaks off to ask again
which is the lady of the house.

75 *I would be loath to* – "I should not
want to".

76 *besides that* – "apart from the fact
that".

77 *con it* – "learn it by heart".

78 *let me sustain no scorn* – "do not
laugh at me". They have begun to
laugh at "him" because "he" is
beginning to repeat Orsino's ex-
pressions of love without any
feeling of his own.

79 *I am very comptible . . . usage* – "I
am very quick to call people to
account (*comptible*) for even the
smallest impoliteness (*sinister
usage*)".

80 *studied* – "learnt by heart", as an
actor learns his part in a play. The
idea that Viola is acting a part is
referred to a number of times in
the following lines, e.g. at line 160.

81 *out of my part* – "not in my
speech".

82 *modest assurance* – "some small
indication".

83 *my profound heart* – "my wise
friend". *Heart* was used as a word
to address a person by; see, for
example, II.iii.14: *How now, my
hearts!*

84 *by the very fangs of malice* – "against
the most ill-willed explanation".

85 *If I do not usurp myself* – "Unless I
hold a position to which I have no
right". This is Olivia's way of
saying that she is indeed the lady
of the house; but Viola treats her
remark literally.

86 *you do usurp . . . to reserve* – "you
have no right to your position
(since Orsino should be the head
of your house), for what you have
to give away (*bestow*) you have no
right to hold back (*reserve*)".

87 *from my commission* – "not part of
my instructions".

OLIVIA

Speak to me; I shall answer for her. Your will?[74]

VIOLA

Most radiant, exquisite, and unmatchable beauty – I pray you, tell me if this be the lady of the house, for I never saw her; I 150 would be loath to[75] cast away my speech; for besides that[76] it is excellently well penned, I have taken great pains to con it.[77] Good beauties, let me sustain no scorn;[78] I am very comptible, even to the least sinister usage.[79]

OLIVIA

Whence came you, sir?   155

VIOLA

I can say little more than I have studied,[80] and that question's out of my part.[81] Good gentle one, give me modest assurance[82] if you be the lady of the house, that I may proceed in my speech.

OLIVIA

Are you a comedian?   160

VIOLA

No, my profound heart;[83] and yet, by the very fangs of malice[84] I swear I am not that I play. Are you the lady of the house?

OLIVIA

If I do not usurp myself,[85] I am.

VIOLA

Most certain, if you are she, you *do* usurp yourself; for what is yours to bestow is not yours to reserve.[86] But this is from my 165 commission;[87] I will on with my speech in your praise, and then show you the heart of my message.

47

88 *I forgive you* – "I excuse you from repeating".

89 *like* – "likely".

90 *feigned* – "false", because it comes from the head, not the heart.

91 *allowed your approach* – "(I) permitted you to come".

92 *not that time . . . me* – "I am not in the humour"; it was thought that the condition of the moon affected people's tempers.

93 *make one* – "take one part" (in the conversation).

94 *skipping* – "foolish".

95 *hoist sail* – "pull up your sails", i.e. go away, as if Viola were a ship. Viola takes up the idea of a ship by calling Maria *swabber* (a seaman who cleans the decks) in the next line.

96 *I am to hull here* – "I must float here with the wind", i.e. not put up sail and go.

97 *Some mollification for your giant* – "Please do something to quieten your 'giant'". Viola makes fun of Maria, who, although she is apparently there to protect Olivia, is in fact small in body; see II.v.11: *Here comes the little villain.*

98 *courtesy* – "polite formality".

99 *fearful* – "frightening", because it is so formal.

100 *your office* – "what you have been told to say".

101 *overture* – "declaration".

102 *taxation* – "demand".

103 *olive*; the olive branch was a sign of peace.

OLIVIA

Come to what is important in 't; I forgive you[88] the praise.

VIOLA

Alas! I took great pains to study it, and 't is poetical.

OLIVIA

It is the more like[89] to be feigned;[90] I pray you keep it in. I heard 170
you were saucy at my gates, and allowed your approach,[91] rather
to wonder at you than to hear you. If you be not mad, be gone;
if you have reason, be brief; 't is not that time of moon with
me[92] to make one[93] in so skipping[94] a dialogue.

MARIA

Will you hoist sail,[95] sir? here lies your way. 175

VIOLA

[To MARIA] No, good swabber; I am to hull here[96] a little longer. [To OLIVIA] Some mollification for your giant,[97] sweet
lady.

OLIVIA

Tell me your mind.

VIOLA

I am a messenger. 180

OLIVIA

Sure, you have some hideous matter to deliver, when the courtesy[98] of it is so fearful.[99] Speak your office.[100]

VIOLA

It alone concerns your ear. I bring no overture[101] of war, no
taxation[102] of homage; I hold the olive[103] in my hand; my words
are as full of peace as matter. 185

49

104 *my entertainment* – "the way I was received" (by Maria, Sir Toby, and Malvolio).

105 *maidenhead* – "the condition of being a maiden".

106 *text.* Olivia plays on Viola's mention of divinity. The *text* would introduce the subject of a religious talk; *doctrine* in line 193 suggests the teaching of religion, and *chapter* in line 196 a part of the Bible.

107 *comfortable* – "comforting".

108 *bosom* – "heart".

109 *by the method* – "according to the plan of your metaphors", i.e. in the language of religion.

110 *the first*, i.e. the first chapter (of a book of the Bible) and the foremost place (in Orsino's heart).

111 *heresy* – "false religious teaching", not the *doctrine* of line 193.

OLIVIA

Yet you began rudely. What are you? What would you?

VIOLA

The rudeness that hath appeared in me have I learned from my
entertainment.[104] What I am, and what I would, are as secret as
maidenhead;[105] to your ears, divinity; to any other's, profanation.

OLIVIA

Give us the place alone; we will hear this divinity.   190
                              [Exeunt MARIA *and* Attendants
Now, sir; what is your text?[106]

VIOLA

Most sweet lady –

OLIVIA

A comfortable[107] doctrine, and much may be said of it. Where
lies your text?

VIOLA

In Orsino's bosom.[108]   195

OLIVIA

In his bosom! In what chapter of his bosom?

VIOLA

To answer by the method,[109] in the first[110] of his heart.

OLIVIA

O! I have read it; it is heresy.[111] Have you no more to say?

VIOLA

Good madam, let me see your face.

112 *out of your text* – "away from the text of your speech".

113 *such a one I was this present* – "this is how I looked just now (while you were talking to me)".

114 *if God did all* – "if it is all done by nature", not make-up.

115 *in grain* – "stained, not to be washed out".

116 *blent* – "blended, mixed well together" (of colours).

117 *cunning* – "clever".

118 *she* – "woman".

119 *no copy*, i.e. no children who will receive your beauties from you, so that they are not lost to the world.

120 *divers* – "various".

121 *labelled to my will* – "attached (as a list) to my will".

122 *indifferent* – "fairly".

123 *praise* here means both "tell a person good about himself" and, as a form of *appraise*, "judge the value of".

124 *if you were . . . are fair* – "even if you were the devil, (I should have to admit) you were beautiful".

125 *such love* (line 219) *. . . beauty* – "such love (as Orsino's) could only be rewarded (by your love in return) (*be but recompensed*) even if you were the crowned queen of beauty without equal (*The nonpareil of beauty*)".

OLIVIA

Have you any commission from your lord to negotiate with my 200
face? You are now out of your text;[112] but we will draw the curtain and show you the picture. Look you, sir; such a one I was
this present;[113] is 't not well done?   [*Unveiling*

VIOLA

Excellently done, if God did all.[114]

OLIVIA

'T is in grain,[115] sir; 't will endure wind and weather.   205

VIOLA

'T is beauty truly blent,[116] whose red and white
Nature's own sweet and cunning[117] hand laid on;
Lady, you are the cruell'st she[118] alive,
If you will lead these graces to the grave
And leave the world no copy.[119]   210

OLIVIA

O, sir, I will not be so hard-hearted! I will give out divers[120]
schedules of my beauty; it shall be inventoried, and every par-
ticle and utensil labelled to my will,[121] as, *Item*, Two lips indifferent[122] red; *Item*, Two grey eyes with lids to them; *Item*,
One neck, one chin, and so forth. Were you sent hither to 215
praise[123] me?

VIOLA

I see you what you are; you are too proud;
But, if you were the devil, you are fair.[124]
My lord and master loves you; O! such love
Could be but recompensed, though you were crowned   220
The nonpareil of beauty.[125]

53

126 *Of great estate* – "very rich".
127 *In voices well divulged* – "well spoken of by people".
128 *dimension* – "form (of body)".
129 *in my master's flame* – "with the burning passion of my master".
130 *a deadly life* – "a life about to be lost (for love)".
131 *Make me a willow cabin* – "Make for myself a shelter under the willow tree"; the "weeping willow" was taken to represent unhappy love.

132 *my soul* – "the one I love", i.e. Olivia.
133 *cantons* – "songs".
134 *reverberate* – "echoing".
135 *rest Between . . . earth* – "be living on the earth". It was considered that all matter was made up of one or more elements, viz. water, fire, air, and earth.

54

OLIVIA

How does he love me?

VIOLA

With adorations, fertile tears,
With groans that thunder love, with sighs of fire.

OLIVIA

Your lord does know my mind; I cannot love him;
Yet I suppose him virtuous, know him noble,   225
Of great estate,[126] of fresh and stainless youth;
In voices well divulged,[127] free, learned, and valiant;
And in dimension[128] and the shape of nature
A gracious person; but yet I cannot love him;
He might have took his answer long ago.   230

VIOLA

If I did love you in my master's flame,[129]
With such a suffering, such a deadly life,[130]
In your denial I would find no sense;
I would not understand it.

OLIVIA

Why, what would you?

VIOLA

Make me a willow cabin[131] at your gate,   235
And call upon my soul[132] within the house;
Write loyal cantons[133] of contemnéd love,
And sing them loud even in the dead of night;
Holla your name to the reverberate[134] hills,
And make the babbling gossip of the air   240
Cry out "Olivia!" O, you should not rest
Between the elements of air and earth,[135]
But you should pity me.

55

136 *You might do much. You* is in contrast to *Your lord* in line 224. Olivia
has been very impressed by Viola's
fiery speech.

137 *my fortunes* – "my present position"; "his" family (*parentage* in
line 244) is nobler than "his"
position as a page would suggest.

138 *your pains* – "the trouble you have
taken (to come)".

139 *fee'd post* – "paid messenger".

140 *Love make . . . love* – "May Love
give the man *you* love a heart of
stone".

141 *cruelty* – "cruel one".

142 *Do give . . . blazon* – "serve you as
a coat of arms (*blazon*) with five
markings on it"; the five qualities
she has just mentioned suggest a
noble upbringing.

143 *Unless . . . the man . . .* Olivia's
exact meaning is not clear, since
she leaves the sentence unfinished,
but she is perhaps thinking: "(I
could not marry Orsino) unless he
were the same as this man . . ."

144 *Even so quickly . . . plague* – "Can
one catch the plague (of love) just
as quickly as this?"

145 *To creep. To* would be omitted in
Modern English: "I feel this
youth's perfections (line 263) . . .
creep in".

five-fold blazon[142]

OLIVIA

You might do much.[136] What is your parentage?

VIOLA

Above my fortunes,[137] yet my state is well;   245
I am a gentleman.

OLIVIA

      Get you to your lord;
I cannot love him. Let him send no more,
Unless, perchance, *you* come to me again,
To tell me how he takes it. Fare you well;
I thank you for your pains;[138] [*She gives* VIOLA *a bag of
  money*] spend this for me.   250

VIOLA

I am no fee'd post,[139] lady; keep your purse;
My master, not myself, lacks recompense.
Love make his heart of flint that you shall love,[140]
And let your fervour, like my master's, be
Placed in contempt! Farewell, fair cruelty.[141]   255
                           [*Exit*

OLIVIA

"What is your parentage?"
"Above my fortunes, yet my state is well;
I am a gentleman." I 'll be sworn thou art;
Thy tongue, thy face, thy limbs, actions, and spirit,
Do give thee five-fold blazon.[142] Not too fast; soft! soft! –   260
Unless the master were the man . . .[143] How now!
Even so quickly may one catch the plague?[144]
Methinks I feel this youth's perfections,
With an invisible and subtle stealth
To creep[145] in at mine eyes. Well, let it be.   265
What, ho! Malvolio!

146 *peevish* – "rude".
147 *county's* – "count's".
148 *Would I or not* – "whether I wanted it or not".
149 *Desire him not . . . lord* – "Tell him not to give his lord any hopeful ideas (*flatter*) (of his chances)".

150 *If that* – "If".
151 *Hie thee* – "Hurry away".
152 *ourselves we do not owe* – "we do not own (*owe*) ourselves"; fate is our master.

Re-enter MALVOLIO

MALVOLIO
Here, madam, at your service.

OLIVIA
Run after that same peevish[146] messenger,
The county's[147] man; he left this ring behind him,
Would I or not;[148] tell him I 'll none of it.
Desire him not to flatter with his lord,[149]   270
Nor hold him up with hopes; I am not for him.
If that[150] the youth will come this way tomorrow,
I 'll give him reasons for 't. Hie thee,[151] Malvolio.

MALVOLIO
Madam, I will.   [*Exit*

OLIVIA
I do I know not what, and fear to find   275
Mine eye too great a flatterer for my mind.
Fate, show thy force; ourselves we do not owe;[152]
What is decreed must be, and be this so.

[*Exit*

(ii.i) Viola's brother Sebastian also escaped drowning, and has now fallen in with another captain, Antonio. Sebastian wishes to be alone, but the captain determines to follow him to Orsino's court, even though this will be at great risk to himself.

1 *nor will you not . . . you?* – "and do you not want me to go with you either?"

2 *By your patience* – "If you will be patient with me (for giving this reply)".

3 *My stars shine darkly* – "I am unlucky". (See note 49 to I.iii.)

4 *malignancy* – "ill-luck", as shown by the stars.

5 *distemper* – "disturb".

6 *were* – "would be".

7 *sooth* – "truly".

8 *my determinate voyage . . . extravagancy* – "the journey I have decided upon is nothing but (*mere*) wandering about (*extravagancy*)".

9 *I am willing to keep in* – "I want to keep to myself".

10 *it charges me . . . express myself* – "politeness compels me (*charges me*), on the contrary, to make myself known".

11 *which I called Roderigo*, i.e. he had, up to then, given his name as Roderigo.

12 *Messaline* may stand for *Mitylene*, but is otherwise unknown.

13 *in an hour* – "within one hour"; they were twins.

14 *would we had so ended* – "I wish we could have ended in the same way". i.e. both died at the same time.

15 *some hour* – "about an hour".

16 *the breach* – "the place where the waves break".

17 *Alas the day!* "O, that I have lived to see this day!"

60

ACT TWO

Scene I. The Sea-coast.
Enter ANTONIO *and* SEBASTIAN.

ANTONIO

Will you stay no longer, nor will you not that I go with you?[1]

SEBASTIAN

By your patience,[2] no. My stars shine darkly[3] over me; the
malignancy[4] of my fate might, perhaps, distemper[5] yours;
therefore I shall crave of you your leave that I may bear my evils
alone. It were[6] a bad recompense for your love, to lay any of   5
them on you.

ANTONIO

Let me yet know of you whither you are bound.

SEBASTIAN

No, sooth,[7] sir; my determinate voyage is mere extravagancy.[8]
But I perceive in you so excellent a touch of modesty, that you
will not extort from me what I am willing to keep in;[9] there-   10
fore it charges me in manners the rather to express myself.[10]
You must know of me then, Antonio, my name is Sebastian,
which I called Roderigo.[11] My father was that Sebastian of
Messaline,[12] whom I know you have heard of. He left behind
him myself and a sister, both born in an hour;[13] if the heavens   15
had been pleased, would we had so ended![14] but you, sir, altered
that; for some hour[15] before you took me from the breach[16]
of the sea was my sister drowned.

ANTONIO

Alas the day![17]

61

18 *was yet . . . beautiful* – "who was yet
considered (*accounted*) beautiful by
many people". A part of the story
depends upon this likeness between
Sebastian and Viola.

19 *such estimable wonder* – "admiration
that judges so highly".

20 *overfar believe* – "go too far in
believing".

21 *publish her* – "make her known".

22 *that Envy . . . call fair* – "that even
Envy (which is unlikely to praise a
person's beauty of mind) would
have to (*could not but*) call beautiful".

23 *more* – "more salt water", i.e. his
tears.

24 *your bad entertainment* – "the poor
way in which you have been received". He has learnt that Sebastian is a person of importance.

25 *your trouble* – "the trouble you have
been caused (by me)".

26 *If you will not . . . love* – "If you do
not want to kill me through my
love (for you)"; Antonio now likes
Sebastian so much that he says he
will die if he is not allowed to serve
him.

27 *kindness* – "tender feelings".

28 *I am yet so near* (line 31) *. . . tales of
me* – "I am still (*yet*) so near to my
mother that on the smallest further
cause my eyes will tell tales of me";
the loss of his sister is so recent that
he will cry.

29 *gentleness* – "good will".

30 *I have many enemies.* Antonio explains later (III.iii lines 26 ff.) that at
one time he fought against Orsino's
ships, and was in some way ro
sponsible for the treasure taken from
them.

SEBASTIAN

A lady, sir, though it was said she much resembled me, was yet   20
of many accounted beautiful;[18] but, though I could not with
such estimable wonder[19] overfar believe[20] that, yet thus far I will
boldly publish her:[21] she bore a mind that Envy could not but
call fair.[22] She is drowned already, sir, with salt water, though
I seem to drown her remembrance again with more.[23]   25

ANTONIO

Pardon me, sir, your bad entertainment.[24]

SEBASTIAN

O good Antonio! forgive me your trouble.[25]

ANTONIO

If you will not murder me for my love,[26] let me be your servant.

SEBASTIAN

If you will not undo what you have done, that is, kill him
whom you have recovered, desire it not. Fare ye well at once;   30
my bosom is full of kindness;[27] and I am yet so near the manners
of my mother that upon the least occasion more mine eyes will
tell tales of me.[28] I am bound to the Count Orsino's court;
farewell.

[*Exit*

ANTONIO

The gentleness[29] of all the gods go with thee.   35
I have many enemies[30] in Orsino's court,
Else would I very shortly see thee there;
But, come what may, I do adore thee so,
That danger shall seem sport, and I will go.

[*Exit*

(II.ii) Malvolio overtakes Viola and gives her the ring from Olivia. She refuses to take it, but realizes that Olivia has fallen in love with her as the boy "Cesario".

1 *following*. At the end of I.v Olivia sent Malvolio after Viola with a ring which, she said, Viola had left behind.

2 *even now* – "just now".

3 *on a moderate pace* – "at a medium rate of walking".

4 *to have taken* – "by having taken".

5 *a desperate assurance* – "a certainty, in which there is no hope (of change), that . . ."

6 *she will none of him* – "she will have nothing to do with him". (Compare note 38 to I.iii.)

7 *so hardy to* – "so bold as to".

8 *She took the ring of me*. This is not true, of course, but Viola has understood the situation, and quickly enters into the falsehood so as not to give away what she has guessed of Olivia.

9 *peevishly* – "rudely".

10 *in your eye* – "where you can see it".

11 *Fortune forbid . . . charmed her!* – "Fortune forbid that my appearance has charmed her (into falling in love with me)".

12 *She made good view of me* – "She looked at me very closely".

13 *her eyes had lost her tongue* – "her eyes made her lose control of her tongue"; what she saw made her speak *in starts distractedly* (line 18).

14 *the cunning . . . messenger* – "her passion has, by cunning, led her to invite me, through this rude messenger, (to visit her again)".

Scene II. A Street.
Enter VIOLA; MALVOLIO *following*[1].

MALVOLIO

Were you not even now[2] with the Countess Olivia?

VIOLA

Even now, sir; on a moderate pace[3] I have since arrived but
hither.

MALVOLIO

She returns this ring to you, sir; you might have saved me my
pains, to have taken[4] it away yourself. She adds, moreover, that   5
you should put your lord into a desperate assurance[5] she will
none of him.[6] And one thing more: that you be never so hardy
to[7] come again in his affairs, unless it be to report your lord's
taking of this. Receive it so. [*He throws the ring on the ground*

VIOLA

She took the ring of me;[8] I 'll none of it.   10

MALVOLIO

Come, sir, you peevishly[9] threw it to her; and her will is it
should be so returned; if it be worth stooping for, there it lies in
your eye;[10] if not, be it his that finds it.

[*Exit*

VIOLA

I left no ring with her; what means this lady?
Fortune forbid my outside have not charmed her![11]   15
She made good view of me;[12] indeed so much
That sure methought her eyes had lost her tongue,[13]
For she did speak in starts distractedly.
She loves me, sure; the cunning of her passion
Invites me in this churlish messenger.[14]   20

65

15 *she were better* – "it would be better for her to ..."
16 *the pregnant enemy* – "the enemy (of men), always full of ideas", i.e. the devil.
17 *the proper-false* – "men who are at once good-looking and deceiving".
18 *In women's waxen ... forms* – "to stamp their images (*set their forms*) in the soft hearts of women"; the metaphor is of sealing or pressing a figure in wax.

19 *fadge* – "turn out".
20 *monster* – "strange creature", both man and woman.
21 *fond as much on him* – "love him as much".
22 *desperate* – "hopeless". Playing the part of a man, she has no hope of winning Orsino's love.
23 *thriftless sighs.* All Olivia's sighs for her will be in vain (*thriftless*), since she is herself a woman.

I hate it as an unfilled can[4]

(II.iii) Sir Toby and Sir Andrew are enjoying themselves drinking together, and Feste, the clown, joins in and sings for them. They become so noisy that Maria and then Malvolio come in and order them to be quiet. When Malvolio has gone, Maria explains a trick she wants to play on him: she will write a letter in Olivia's handwriting which will suggest to Malvolio that his lady is in love with him.

1 *a-bed* – "in bed".
2 *betimes* – "early".
3 *diluculo surgere* (Latin) – "to get up at day-break (is most healthful)". These are the first two words of a Latin phrase from a school-book of Shakespeare's time, which every educated person would have known. Sir Andrew says, "I know not" in the next line.

4 *an unfilled can*, i.e. a can not filled up with wine.
5 *the four elements*, earth, air, fire, and water, were thought to be the base of everything in existence; a person's character was decided by the way in which these "elements" were mixed together in him. (Compare note 135 to I.v.)

None of my lord's ring! Why, he sent her none.
I am the man; if it be so, as 't is,
Poor lady, she were better[15] love a dream.
Disguise, I see thou art a wickedness
Wherein the pregnant enemy[16] does much.   25
How easy is it for the proper-false[17]
In women's waxen hearts to set their forms![18]
Alas! our frailty is the cause, not we,
For such as we are made of, such we be.
How will this fadge?[19] My master loves her dearly;   30
And I, poor monster,[20] fond as much on him;[21]
And she, mistaken, seems to dote on me.
What will become of this? As I am man,
My state is desperate[22] for my master's love;
As I am woman – now alas the day! –   35
What thriftless sighs[23] shall poor Olivia breathe!
O time, thou must untangle this, not I;
It is too hard a knot for me to untie.

                                      [Exit

Scene III. *A Room in Olivia's House.*

Enter SIR TOBY BELCH *and* SIR ANDREW AGUECHEEK.

SIR TOBY

Approach, Sir Andrew: not to be a-bed[1] after midnight is to be up betimes;[2] and *diluculo surgere*,[3] thou knowest –

SIR ANDREW

Nay, by my troth, I know not; but I know, to be up late is to be up late.

SIR TOBY

A false conclusion; I hate it as an unfilled can.[4] To be up after   5
midnight, and to go to bed then, is early; so that to go to bed
after midnight is to go to bed betimes. Does not our life con-
sist of the four elements?[5]

67

6 *Thou 'rt a scholar*; this is an empty compliment, certain to amuse the audience, since he did not recognize the well-known Latin phrase just repeated by Sir Toby.

7 *Marian* is a form of *Maria*; she is also called *Mistress Mary* (line 105).

8 *my hearts* – "my good friends".

9 *the picture of "we three"* was an inn-sign with *two* wooden heads painted on it; the person looking at the sign is supposed to be the third wooden head, i.e. fool. Sir Andrew calls the Clown a fool, and the Clown suggests they are all fools.

10 *catch* – a song for three or more voices.

11 *breast* – "voice to sing with".

12 *leg*, i.e. the leg which he shows when he bows to his audience after singing.

13 *Pigrogromitus, Vapians, Queubus* (line 21) are invented names which Feste brought in to show his listeners that he pretended to a knowledge of the Latin authors. This passage has no meaning, and the joke is that Sir Andrew should think it good fooling. The same applies to Feste's following lines 23–25.

14 *leman* – "sweetheart".

15 *impeticos thy gratillity*. These are nonsense forms of other words, perhaps "impetticoat thy gratuity", i.e. "put your gift into my sweetheart's coat pocket".

16 *Malvolio's nose* (line 23) ... *bottle-ale houses*. This is again nonsense, but the Clown may possibly have been thinking in this way: "I 'll pocket your gift; Malvolio is sharp in nosing out faults, and would know if I stole drink from the house; my sweetheart is a fine lady, whom I must take to drink at (an inn called) 'The Myrmidons', which is an expensive place"; *whipstock* – "the handle of a whip"; the *Myrmidons* were the attendants of Achilles, and here perhaps are imagined as pictures on the sign of an inn; *bottle-ale* suggests cheap drink.

17 *when all is done* – "after all".

SIR ANDREW

Faith, so they say; but I think it rather consists of eating and
drinking.   10

SIR TOBY

Thou 'rt a scholar;[6] let us therefore eat and drink. [*Calling*]
Marian,[7] I say! a stoup of wine!

Enter FESTE

SIR ANDREW

Here comes the fool, i' faith.

FESTE

How now, my hearts![8] Did you never see the picture of "we
three"?[9]   15

SIR TOBY

Welcome, ass. Now let 's have a catch.[10]

SIR ANDREW

By my troth, the fool has an excellent breast.[11] I had rather than
forty shillings I had such a leg,[12] and so sweet a breath to sing,
as the fool has. [*To* FESTE] In sooth, thou wast in very gracious
fooling last night, when thou spokest of Pigrogromitus,[13] of the   20
Vapians passing the equinoctial of Queubus; 't was very good, i'
faith. I sent thee sixpence for thy leman;[14] hadst it?

FESTE

I did impeticos thy gratillity,[15] for Malvolio's nose is no whipstock; my lady has a white hand, and the Myrmidons are no
bottle-ale houses.[16]   25

SIR ANDREW

Excellent! Why, this is the best fooling, when all is done.[17]
Now, a song.

18 *testril of me* – "a sixpenny piece from me".

19 *give a –*. The Clown interrupts Sir Andrew, who is about to make another commonplace remark, perhaps, "if one knight give, another should too". Much of Sir Andrew's stupidity is shown in his habit of accepting other people's remarks as true or just and generalising on them; see, for example, I.iii.92 ff., and lines 30–32 of the present scene.

20 *sweeting* – "sweet one".

21 *'t is not hereafter* – "it is not a matter for the future".

22 *In delay . . . plenty* – "there is no advantage in delaying".

23 *sweet-and-twenty* – "darling", perhaps "sweet, and twenty years old".

24 *will* – "which will".

70

SIR TOBY

Come on; there is sixpence for you; let 's have a song.

SIR ANDREW

There 's a testril of me too;[18] if one knight give a –[19]

FESTE

Would you have a love-song, or a song of good life?   30

SIR TOBY

A love-song, a love-song.

SIR ANDREW

Ay, ay; I care not for good life.

FESTE [*sings*]

O mistress mine! where are you roaming?
O stay and hear! your true love 's coming,
   That can sing both high and low.   35
Trip no further, pretty sweeting;[20]
Journeys end in lovers meeting,
   Every wise man's son doth know.

SIR ANDREW

Excellent good, i' faith.

SIR TOBY

Good, good.   40

FESTE [*sings*]

What is love? 'T is not hereafter;[21]
Present mirth hath present laughter;
   What 's to come is still unsure.
In delay there lies no plenty;[22]
Then come kiss me, sweet-and-twenty,[23]   45
   Youth 's a stuff will[24] not endure.

71

25 *A contagious breath* – "A good song, which attracted me (*contagious*)".

26 *contagious*. Sir Andrew catches up the high-sounding word; and then, to make further nonsense, Sir Toby takes it literally in the following line.

27 *To hear by . . . in contagion* – "(A strange idea) to hear through the nose (like catching a contagious fever by breathing bad air)! But the song (*it*) is indeed contagiously sweet (*dulcet*)".

28 *make the welkin dance* – "drink till the sky (*welkin*) seems to turn round".

29 *will draw . . . weaver.* Fine music affects people deeply; Shakespeare speaks of it elsewhere as drawing men's souls from their bodies. Weavers were considered to be very serious people who sang only church music. Sir Toby says that his catch will affect even weavers very deeply; it will "draw three souls" out of each one.

30 *dog at* – "very good at".

31 *By 'r lady* – "By Our Lady", i.e. the Virgin Mary.

32 *some dogs will catch well.* The Clown plays, not very successfully, on Sir Andrew's phrase *dog at* and the word *catch*.

33 "*Thou knave*" is the name of the catch. Each singer sings the same tune, but at a different time from the rest. It also seems in the song that at the end of his line each singer in turn addresses another as *thou knave*, and this is why the Clown will have to call Sir Andrew *knave* (lines 57–8) while they sing it.

34 *Hold thy peace* – "Keep quiet".

35 *one* – "someone".

72

SIR ANDREW

A mellifluous voice, as I am true knight.

SIR TOBY

A contagious breath.[25]

SIR ANDREW

Very sweet and contagious,[26] i' faith.

SIR TOBY

To hear by the nose, it is dulcet in contagion.[27] But shall we   50
make the welkin dance[28] indeed? Shall we rouse the night-owl in
a catch that will draw three souls out of one weaver?[29] Shall we
do that?

SIR ANDREW

An you love me, let 's do 't; I am dog at[30] a catch.

FESTE

By 'r lady,[31] sir, and some dogs will catch well.[32]   55

SIR ANDREW

Most certain. Let our catch be, "Thou knave".[33]

FESTE

"Hold thy peace,[34] thou knave", knight? I shall be constrained
in 't to call thee knave, knight.

SIR ANDREW

'T is not the first time I have constrained one[35] to call me
knave. Begin, fool; it begins "Hold thy peace".   60

FESTE

I shall never begin if I hold my peace.

36 *Cataian* – apparently "rogue", literally one who lives in *Cathay*, i.e. China.

37 *politicians* – "dishonest men"; Shakespeare uses the word *politician* usually in a bad sense.

38 *Peg-a-Ramsey*, used here as a term of abuse, is the name of an old song.

39 "*Three merry men be we*" is the verse-ending of a once-popular song.

40 *Tillyvally; lady!* – "Nonsense; lady, indeed!", in reply to Maria's words about "my lady" in line 63. And the word *lady* reminds him of a song with *lady* repeated in it; he begins to sing it in the next line.

41 *Beshrew me* – "Indeed".

42 *natural* for *naturally*; but the audience would take *natural* to mean also "like a fool".

43 *O! the twelfth day* . . . The words of this song are now lost.

44 *honesty* – "sense of what is proper".

45 *but to gabble like tinkers* – "to prevent you from gabbling like tinkers", who were considered to be great talkers and drinkers.

74

SIR ANDREW

Good, i' faith. Come, begin.

[They sing a catch

Enter MARIA

MARIA

What a caterwauling do you keep here! If my lady have not
called up her steward Malvolio and bid him turn you out of
doors, never trust me.   65

SIR TOBY

My lady's a Cataian;[36] we are politicians;[37] Malvolio's a Peg-a-
Ramsey,[38] and "Three merry men be we".[39] Am not I consan-
guineous? Am I not of her blood? Tillyvally; lady![40] *[Singing]*
There dwelt a man in Babylon, lady, lady! –

FESTE

Beshrew me,[41] the knight's in admirable fooling.   70

SIR ANDREW

Ay, he does well enough if he be disposed, and so do I too.; he
does it with a better grace, but I do it more natural.[42]

SIR TOBY

[Singing] O! the twelfth day of December –[43]

MARIA

For the love o' God, peace!

Enter MALVOLIO

MALVOLIO

My masters, are you mad, or what are you? Have you no wit,   75
manners, nor honesty,[44] but to gabble like tinkers[45] at this time
of night? Do ye make an alehouse of my lady's house, that ye

46 *coziers' catches* – "shoe-menders' songs".

47 *remorse* – "sparing".

48 *keep time* – "keep up a regular beat" (in music).

49 *Sneck up!* – "Go hang!"

50 *round* – "open in speech".

51 *harbours you* – "gives you a home here".

52 *nothing allied to your disorders* – "in no way connected with your bad behaviour". She is connected with him in family but not *allied* to his conduct.

53 *separate yourself . . . misdemeanours* – "free yourself from your bad conduct". Malvolio's style of speaking is purposely strange, so that Sir Toby may be made to look foolish.

54 *Farewell, dear heart* begins a song which Sir Toby is reminded of by Malvolio's use of the word *farewell* (line 87). Sir Toby and Feste then sing lines of the song in turn, and Maria and Malvolio interrupt them. The original song is addressed to a lady, but they make it apply to Malvolio.

76

squeak out your coziers' catches[46] without any mitigation or remorse[47] of voice? Is there no respect of place, persons, nor time
in you?   80

SIR TOBY

We did keep time,[48] sir, in our catches. Sneck up![49]

MALVOLIO

Sir Toby, I must be round[50] with you. My lady bade me tell
you that, though she harbours you[51] as her kinsman, she's
nothing allied to your disorders.[52] If you can separate yourself
and your misdemeanours,[53] you are welcome to the house;   85
if not, an it would please you to take leave of her, she is very
willing to bid you farewell.

SIR TOBY

[Singing] *Farewell, dear heart,*[54] *since I must needs be gone.*

MARIA

Nay, good Sir Toby.

FESTE

[Singing] *His eyes do show his days are almost done.*   90

MALVOLIO

Is 't even so?

SIR TOBY

[Singing] *But I will never die.*

FESTE

Sir Toby, there you lie.

MALVOLIO

This is much credit to you.

SIR TOBY

[Singing in turn]   *Shall I bid him go?*   95

55 *Out o' tune.* It is apparently the fourth *no* in line 98 which is "out of tune", since there are only three noes in the original song.

56 *ye lie.* The Clown lies when he sings that Sir Toby dare not bid Malvolio go.

57 *cakes and ale*; these were food and drink for holidays, and the phrase came to mean "good living". Malvolio as a puritan would naturally dislike them.

58 *by Saint Anne.* The Clown swears by a saint so as to annoy the puritan Malvolio.

59 *ginger* is apparently mentioned because it was thought to bring on love.

60 *rub your chain with crumbs.* Malvolio, as steward in Olivia's house, wears a gold chain to distinguish him from the other servants; objects made from precious metal used to be cleaned with bread-crumbs.

61 *give means for this uncivil rule* – "give the means (i.e. the drink) for these disorderly parties".

62 *shake your ears*, like a donkey.

63 *to challenge him the field* – "to challenge him to fight".

Go, sir, rub your chain with crumbs[60]

78

FESTE

What an if you do?

SIR TOBY

Shall I bid him go, and spare not?

FESTE

O! no, no, no, no, you dare not.

SIR TOBY

[*To* FESTE] Out o' tune,[55] sir! ye lie.[56] [*To* MALVOLIO] Art any
more than a steward? Dost thou think, because thou art vir-   100
tuous, there shall be no more cakes and ale?[57]

FESTE

Yes, by Saint Anne;[58] and ginger[59] shall be hot i' the mouth too.

SIR TOBY

[*To* FESTE] Thou 'rt i' the right. [*To* MALVOLIO] Go, sir, rub
your chain with crumbs.[60] A stoup of wine, Maria!

MALVOLIO

Mistress Mary, if you prized my lady's favour at any thing more   105
than contempt, you would not give means for this uncivil
rule;[61] she shall know of it, by this hand.

[*Exit*

MARIA

Go shake your ears.[62]

SIR ANDREW

'T were as good a deed as to drink when a man 's a-hungry, to   110
challenge him the field,[63] and then to break promise with him
and make a fool of him.

79

64 *For* – "As for".

65 *gull him into a nayword* – "make such a fool of him that his name will become a proverbial word (*nayword*) (for a fool)".

66 *recreation* – "object to be laughed at".

67 *Possess us* – "Let us know (your plan)".

68 *The devil . . . he is* – "He is not a puritan, by the devil"; she said before (line 122) that he was *a kind of puritan*, suggesting that he was not always puritanical in his manner. This is confirmed in what follows.

69 *time-pleaser* – one who changes his opinions to suit his interests and profit.

70 *affectioned* – "affected".

71 *cons state without book* – "learns by heart fine phrases on state affairs", so that he can use them in conversation.

72 *by great swarths* – "in great quantities"; swarths or swaths are literally lines of cut grass or corn.

73 *the best persuaded of himself* – "a man with the highest opinion of himself".

74 *his ground of faith* – "his firm belief".

75 *that vice* – "that weakness", i.e. his vanity.

SIR TOBY

Do 't, knight; I 'll write thee a challenge; or I 'll deliver thy
indignation to him by word of mouth.

MARIA

Sweet Sir Toby, be patient for tonight; since the youth of the
count's was today with my lady, she is much out of quiet. For[64] 115
Monsieur Malvolio, let me alone with him; if I do not gull him
into a nayword,[65] and make him a common recreation,[66] do not
think I have wit enough to lie straight in my bed. I know I can
do it.

SIR TOBY

Possess us,[67] possess us.   120

SIR ANDREW

Tell us something of him.

MARIA

Marry, sir, sometimes he is a kind of puritan.

SIR ANDREW

O! if I thought that, I 'd beat him like a dog.

SIR TOBY

What, for being a puritan? Thy exquisite reason, dear knight!

SIR ANDREW

I have no exquisite reason for 't, but I have reason good enough. 125

MARIA

The devil a puritan that he is,[68] or any thing constantly, but a
time-pleaser;[69] an affectioned[70] ass, that cons state without
book,[71] and utters it by great swarths;[72] the best persuaded of
himself;[73] so crammed, as he thinks, with excellences, that it is
his ground of faith[74] that all that look on him love him; and on 130
that vice[75] in him will my revenge find notable cause to work.

81

76 *obscure epistles of love* – "love-letters very uncertain in meaning".

77 *expressure* – "expression".

78 *most feelingly personated* – "very closely described". The letters will be written in a hand which looks like Olivia's (lines 136–8), and Malvolio will then be led to believe that his lady is in love with him.

79 *a horse of that colour* – "a matter of that sort".

80 *Ass.* Maria puns on *ass* and *as*.

SIR TOBY

What wilt thou do?

MARIA

I will drop in his way some obscure epistles of love;[76] wherein, by the colour of his beard, the shape of his leg, the manner of his gait, the expressure[77] of his eye, forehead, and complexion, he shall find himself most feelingly personated.[78] I can write very like my lady your niece; on a forgotten matter we can hardly make distinction of our hands.

SIR TOBY

Excellent! I smell a device.

SIR ANDREW

I have 't in my nose, too.

SIR TOBY

He shall think, by the letters that thou wilt drop, that they come from my niece, and that she 's in love with him.

MARIA

My purpose is, indeed, a horse of that colour.[79]

SIR ANDREW

And your horse now would make him an ass.

MARIA

Ass,[80] I doubt not.

SIR ANDREW

O! 't will be admirable.

81 *my physic . . . with him* – "my medicine will take effect on him".

82 *observe his construction of it* – "notice the meaning he puts upon it".

83 *Penthesilea* was queen of the Amazons, the race of giant women. Maria is small, and Sir Toby makes fun of her by giving her the name of an Amazon.

84 *Before me* – "Indeed".

85 *Thou hadst need* – "You must".

86 *recover* – "get".

87 *a foul way out* – "in a bad situation".

88 *call me cut* – "call me a horse", a term of abuse.

89 *burn some sack* – "warm up some wine"; *sack* was the name given to a kind of dry wine.

Good night, Penthesilea[83]

84

MARIA

Sport royal, I warrant you; I know my physic will work with
him.[81] I will plant you two, and let the fool make a third, where
he shall find the letter; observe his construction of it.[82] For this
night, to bed, and dream on the event. Farewell.   150
                                                              [*Exit*

SIR TOBY

Good night, Penthesilea.[83]

SIR ANDREW

Before me,[84] she 's a good wench.

SIR TOBY

She 's a beagle, true-bred, and one that adores me; what o' that?

SIR ANDREW

I was adored once too.

SIR TOBY

Let 's to bed, knight. Thou hadst need[85] send for more money. 155

SIR ANDREW

If I cannot recover[86] your niece, I am a foul way out.[87]

SIR TOBY

Send for money, knight; if thou hast her not i' the end, call me
cut.[88]

SIR ANDREW

If I do not, never trust me, take it how you will.

SIR TOBY

Come, come; I 'll go burn some sack;[89] 't is too late to go to bed 160
now. Come, knight; come knight.
                                                              [*Exeunt*

(II.iv) The Duke calls for more music, and then asks "Cesario" about "his" own feelings of love. Viola suggests in her answers that she is in love with the Duke, but he does not understand her in this way. He sends her once more to woo Olivia.

1 *but* – "nothing but".
2 *antique* – "curious".
3 *passion* – "feelings".
4 *recollected terms* – "carefully worked phrases", which are artificial and not the expression of simple truth.
5 *the while* – "in the meantime".

6 *Unstaid and skittish* (line 16) . . . *is beloved* – "unsure and changeable (*skittish*) in every feeling (*motion*) except that (which lies in) the fixed image of the loved one".
7 *It gives a very echo . . is throned* – "It exactly echoes (in music) the deepest feelings of love".

Scene IV. A Room in the Duke's Palace.
Enter DUKE, VIOLA, CURIO, *and others.*

DUKE

Give me some music. Now, good morrow, friends.
Now, good Cesario, but[1] that piece of song,
That old and antique[2] song we heard last night;
Methought it did relieve my passion[3] much,
More than light airs and recollected terms[4]   5
Of these most brisk and giddy-pacéd times.
Come; but one verse.

CURIO

He is not here, so please your lordship, that should sing it.

DUKE

Who was it?

CURIO

Feste, the jester, my lord; a fool that the lady Olivia's father   10
took much delight in. He is about the house.

DUKE

Seek him out, and play the tune the while.[5]
                                        [*Exit* CURIO. *Music*
Come hither, boy: if ever thou shalt love,
In the sweet pangs of it remember me;
For such as I am all true lovers are,   15
Unstaid and skittish in all motions else
Save in the constant image of the creature
That is beloved.[6] How dost thou like this tune?

VIOLA

It gives a very echo to the seat
Where Love is throned.[7]

87

8 *masterly* – "like a master (in the arts of love and expression)".

9 *stayed upon some favour* – "rested lovingly on some face (*favour*)".

10 *by your favour*, "with your good-will", was a set phrase used when a servant spoke to his master. But the Duke uses *favour* to mean "face", and Viola puns on this, making the phrase also mean "rather near to your face",' since she is secretly in love with him.

11 *Of your complexion* – "She looks like you".

12 *take An elder* – "take (in marriage) someone older".

13 *so wears she to him* – "for by doing so she changes herself to suit him", as clothes become suited to the person who wears them.

14 *sways she level . . . heart* – "she justly rules her husband's affection".

15 *fancies* – "loves".

16 *worn* – "used up".

DUKE

Thou dost speak masterly.[8]   20
My life upon 't, young though thou art, thine eye
Hath stayed upon some favour[9] that it loves;
Hath it not, boy?

VIOLA

A little, by your favour.[10]

DUKE

What kind of woman is 't?

VIOLA

Of your complexion.[11]

DUKE

She is not worth thee, then. What years, i' faith?   25

VIOLA

About your years, my lord.

DUKE

Too old, by heaven. Let still the woman take
An elder[12] than herself, so wears she to him,[13]
So sways she level in her husband's heart;[14]
For, boy, however we do praise ourselves,   30
Our fancies[15] are more giddy and unfirm,
More longing, wavering, sooner lost and worn,[16]
Than women's are.

VIOLA

I think it well, my lord.

89

17 *cannot hold the bent* – "cannot remain firm".
18 *even* – "just".
19 *spinsters* – "women who spin thread".
20 *free* – (perhaps) "unmarried".
21 *Do use to chant it* – "often sing it".
22 *silly sooth* – "simple truth", not in the *recollected terms* of the songs described in line 5.
23 *the old age* – "times long ago".
24 *Come away* – "Come here".
25 *cypress* – "coffin of cypress wood". The cypress tree was associated with death, perhaps because it is dark and black beneath its covering of green leaves.

26 *a fair cruel maid* was very often the subject of songs and poems in Shakespeare's day. The singer or poet, a man, loves a beautiful woman who will not love him in return.
27 *stuck all with yew* – "sprinkled all over with yew leaves".
28 *My part of death . . . share it* – "No one so true (in love) as I has played this part (in the tragedy) of death", i.e. died for love.

And in sad cypress[25] *let me be laid*

DUKE

Then let thy love be younger than thyself,
Or thy affection cannot hold the bent;[17]   35
For women are as roses, whose fair flower
Being once displayed, doth fall that very hour.

yarn
passes
quickly?

VIOLA

And so they are; alas! that they are so;
To die, even[18] when they to perfection grow.

Re-enter CURIO *and* FESTE

DUKE

O, fellow! come, the song we had last night.   40
Mark it, Cesario; it is old and plain;
The spinsters[19] and the knitters in the sun,
And the free[20] maids that weave their thread with bones,
Do use to chant[21] it; it is silly sooth,[22]
And dallies with the innocence of love,   45
Like the old age.[23]

FESTE

Are you ready, sir?

DUKE

Ay; prithee, sing.   [*Music*

FESTE

Come away,[24] come away, death,
   And in sad cypress[25] let me be laid;   50
Fly away, fly away, breath;
   I am slain by a fair cruel maid.[26]
My shroud of white, stuck all with yew,[27]
     O! prepare it;
My part of death, no one so true   55
     Did share it.[28]

29 *strown* (see Glossary under *strew*).

30 *corse* – "body".

31 *thy pains* – "the trouble you have taken (in singing to me)".

32 *paid* – "paid for, suffered for".

33 *leave to leave thee* – "permission to go away from you". The Duke is taking part in the word-play.

34 *the melancholy god;* the god of melancholy may be expected to protect Orsino, who is so melancholy himself.

35 *thy doublet . . . taffeta* – "your coat (*doublet*) of silk cloth which changes colour (according to the way the light falls on it)".

36 *a very opal* – "just like an opal", a stone which also changes colour according to the light. Orsino in love is as changeable in behaviour as these things.

37 *such constancy*, as Orsino's, that is; he has no constancy at all, but is always changing.

38 *their intent everywhere* – "the objects of their journey unfixed".

39 *a good voyage of nothing* – (perhaps) "an interesting voyage out of something ordinary". The clown is apparently suggesting in fun that if more seamen were as changeable in behaviour as Orsino, dull voyages would be made much more interesting.

> Not a flower, not a flower sweet,
>   On my black coffin let there be strown;[29]
> Not a friend, not a friend greet
>   My poor corse,[30] where my bones shall be thrown;   60
> A thousand thousand sighs to save,
>   Lay me O! where
> Sad true lover never find my grave,
>   To weep there.

DUKE

[*Gives him money*] There 's for thy pains.[31]   65

FESTE

No pains, sir; I take pleasure in singing, sir.

DUKE

I 'll pay thy pleasure, then.

FESTE

Truly, sir, and pleasure will be paid,[32] one time or another.

DUKE

Give me now leave to leave thee.[33]

FESTE

Now, the melancholy god[34] protect thee, and the tailor make   70
thy doublet of changeable taffeta,[35] for thy mind is a very opal![36]
I would have men of such constancy[37] put to sea, that their business might be every thing and their intent everywhere;[38] for
that 's it that always makes a good voyage of nothing.[39] Farewell.
                                                    [*Exit*

40 *Let all the rest give place* – "Leave us, all the rest of you". He wants to talk to Viola alone.

41 *yond same sovereign cruelty* – "that queen of cruelty".

42 *parts* – "possessions", e.g. the *dirty lands* of the line before.

43 *I hold . . . fortune* – "I consider as lightly as fortune (which is well known to be changeable)".

44 *pranks her in; prank*, "beautify with jewels", is clearly suggested by *gems* in the line before. Lines 81 and 82 probably mean: "But what attracts my soul is the miracle and queen of jewels which nature beautifies her as", i.e. her beauty of person and character, not her possessions.

45 *Say that* – "Suppose".

46 *retention* – "ability to be constant (in love)".

47 *motion of the liver* – "true feeling", one from the liver, which was taken to be the seat of love. The *palate*, by contrast, rules only passing *appetite*.

48 *cloyment* – "overfilling (with good things)".

49 *revolt* – "distaste".

50 *compare* for *comparison*.

DUKE

Let all the rest give place.[40]

[*Exeunt* CURIO *and* Attendants

              Once more, Cesario,   75
Get thee to yond same sovereign cruelty;[41]
Tell her, my love, more noble than the world,
Prizes not quantity of dirty lands;
The parts[42] that fortune hath bestowed upon her,
Tell her, I hold as giddily as fortune;[43]   80
But 't is that miracle and queen of gems
That nature pranks her in,[44] attracts my soul.

VIOLA

But if she cannot love you, sir?

DUKE

I cannot be so answered.

VIOLA

             Sooth, but you must.
Say that[45] some lady, as perhaps there is,   85
Hath for *your* love as great a pang of heart
As you have for Olivia; you cannot love her;
You tell her so; must she not then be answered?

DUKE

There is no woman's sides
Can bide the beating of so strong a passion   90
As love doth give my heart; no woman's heart
So big, to hold so much; they lack retention.[46]
Alas! their love may be called appetite,
No motion of the liver,[47] but the palate,
That suffer surfeit, cloyment,[48] and revolt;[49]   95
But mine is all as hungry as the sea,
And can digest as much. Make no compare[50]
Between that love a woman can bear me
And that I owe Olivia.

51 *My father had a daughter* . . . Viola is referring to herself, but speaks in this way so as to prevent the Duke from finding out who she is.

52 *A blank*; her history has never been written down.

53 *let concealment . . . cheek; damask –* "red"; "let her silence (on the subject of her love) eat up the redness of youth from her cheek like a worm inside a bud".

54 *a green and yellow melancholy –* "a sadness which made her sick in mind and body".

55 *Patience on a monument –* "a figure of Patience cut on a monument".

56 *Our shows . . . will –* "The passion we show is greater than we wish to put into effect".

57 *yet I know not*; she thinks that her brother Sebastian may be alive after all.

VIOLA

Ay, but I know –

DUKE

What dost thou know?   100

VIOLA

Too well what love women to men may owe;
In faith, they are as true of heart as we.
My father had a daughter[51] loved a man,
As it might be, perhaps, were I a woman,
I should your lordship.

DUKE

And what's her history?   105

VIOLA

A blank,[52] my lord. She never told her love,
But let concealment, like a worm i' the bud,
Feed on her damask cheek,[53] she pined in thought,
And with a green and yellow melancholy,[54]
She sat like Patience on a monument,[55]   110
Smiling at grief. Was not this love indeed?
We men may say more, swear more; but indeed
Our shows are more than will,[56] for still we prove
Much in our vows, but little in our love.

DUKE

But died thy sister of her love, my boy?   115

VIOLA

I am all the daughters of my father's house,
And all the brothers too; and yet I know not.[57]
Sir, shall I to this lady?

58 *denay* – "denial".

(II.v) Maria has written the letter, and now she throws it down for Malvolio to find. He enters, day-dreaming of what might happen if he married Olivia; and then he discovers the letter. What is written in it is not very clear, but he takes it to mean that Olivia has declared her love for him.

1 *Come thy ways, Signior Fabian* – "Come along, Mr Fabian".

2 *sheep-biter* – "dog which worries sheep", and so "a spiteful, sour-tempered man".

3 *come by some notable shame* – "suffer some particular shame".

4 *about a bear-baiting* – "because of a display of bear-baiting", i.e. tying a bear to a post and then setting dogs to annoy it. This cruel sport was popular in Shakespeare's day.

5 *black and blue*; this phrase is perhaps borrowed from "beat him black and blue", i.e. soundly.

6 *it is pity of our lives* – "it would be something to regret all our lives".

7 *metal of India* – "wonderful woman", rare as a precious metal from the East.

you know he brought me out o' favour with my lady about a bear-baiting[4] *here*

DUKE

Ay, that 's the theme.
To her in haste; give her this jewel; say
My love can give no place, bide no denay.[58]   120

[*Exeunt*

Scene V. Olivia's Garden.

Enter SIR TOBY BELCH, SIR ANDREW AGUECHEEK,
and FABIAN.

SIR TOBY

Come thy ways, Signior Fabian.[1]

FABIAN

Nay, I 'll come; if I lose a scruple of this sport, let me be boiled to
death with melancholy.

SIR TOBY

Would'st thou not be glad to have the niggardly, rascally sheep-
biter[2] come by some notable shame?[3]   5

FABIAN

I would exult, man; you know he brought me out o' favour
with my lady about a bear-baiting[4] here.

SIR TOBY

To anger him we ll have the bear again, and we will fool him
black and blue;[5] shall we not, Sir Andrew?

SIR ANDREW

An we do not, it is pity of our lives.[6]   10

Enter MARIA

SIR TOBY

Here comes the little villain. How now, my metal of India?[7]

99

8 *behaviour* – "courtly manners".

9 *contemplative idiot* – "self-deceiving fool".

10 *Close* – "Keep close together, in hiding".

11 *tickling* – a way of catching fish by tickling them underneath.

12 *she did affect me* – "she (Olivia) cared for me".

13 *fancy* – "fall in love".

14 *one of my complexion* – "someone with a nature like mine"; *complexion* – "nature", particularly as shown by the face.

15 *uses* – "treats".

16 *Contemplation* – "Thinking about himself".

17 *he jets . . . plumes* – "he walks about boastfully beneath his raised feathers".

18 *'Slight* is short for "By God's light", an oath.

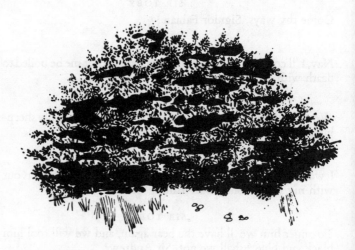

Get ye all three into the box-tree

MARIA

Get ye all three into the box-tree. [*They hide behind the hedge.*]
Malvolio 's coming down this walk; he has been yonder i' the
sun, practising behaviour[8] to his own shadow this half hour. Observe him, for the love of mockery; for I know this letter will   15
make a contemplative idiot[9] of him. Close,[10] in the name of
jesting! Lie thou there; [*She throws down a letter*] for here comes
the trout that must be caught with tickling.[11]

[*Exit*

Enter MALVOLIO

MALVOLIO

'T is but fortune; all is fortune. Maria once told me she did affect
me;[12] and I have heard herself come thus near, that, should she   20
fancy,[13] it should be one of my complexion.[14] Besides, she uses[15]
me with a more exalted respect than any one else that follows
her. What should I think on 't ?

SIR TOBY [*to* SIR ANDREW *and* FABIAN]

Here 's an overweening rogue!

FABIAN

O, peace! Contemplation[16] makes a rare turkey-cock of him;   25
how he jets under his advanced plumes![17]

SIR ANDREW

'Slight,[18] I could so beat the rogue!

SIR TOBY

Peace! I say!

MALVOLIO

To be Count Malvolio!

SIR TOBY

Ah, rogue!   30

SIR ANDREW

Pistol him, pistol him.

101

19 *example* – another example of the same thing happening before, i.e. a noble lady marrying a servant.

20 *of the Strachy*. This phrase has not been explained satisfactorily. *Strachy* may be a family name; it may be a mistake for Malphey, since there was, in Shakespeare's day, a story current about a duchess of Malphey (or Malfi) who married her servant.

21 *the yeoman of the wardrobe* was an upper servant in a great household who looked after the clothes.

22 *Fie on him* – "A curse on him".

23 *Jezebel* – the name of a bad woman in the Bible. Sir Andrew probably thinks she was a man, and makes a characteristic mistake in calling Malvolio after her.

24 *blows him* – "makes him swell (with pride)".

25 *my state* – "my chair of state", as master of the household.

26 *a stone-bow* – a cross-bow from which stones could be shot.

27 *officers* – "servants".

28 *branched* – "decorated with patterns of branches".

29 *to have . . . state* – "to take on and enjoy the grandeur of my position".

30 *a demure travel of regard* – "solemnly looking at them one by one".

31 *I would* – "I wish".

32 *Bolts and shackles* is a curse, meaning, apparently, "(Put him in) bolts and shackles", the fate of a prisoner.

*O! for a stone-bow,*²⁶ *to hit him in the eye*

SIR TOBY

Peace! peace!

MALVOLIO

There is example[19] for 't; the lady of the Strachy[20] married the
yeoman of the wardrobe.[21]

SIR ANDREW

Fie on him,[22] Jezebel![23]   35

FABIAN

O, peace! now he 's deeply in; look how imagination blows
him.[24]

MALVOLIO

Having been three months married to her, sitting in my
state, –[25]

SIR TOBY

O! for a stone-bow,[26] to hit him in the eye.   40

MALVOLIO

Calling my officers[27] about me, in my branched[28] velvet gown;
having come from a day-bed, where I have left Olivia sleeping, –

SIR TOBY

Fire and brimstone!

FABIAN

O, peace! peace!   45

MALVOLIO

And then to have the humour of state;[29] and after a demure
travel of regard,[30] telling them I know my place, as I would[31]
they should do theirs, to ask for my kinsman Toby, –

SIR TOBY

Bolts and shackles![32]

33 *make out* – "go out".
34 *with my* – Malvolio is probably going to say "chain", but remembers that his chain is the sign of his post as steward, which he will no longer hold if he becomes Olivia's husband.
35 *curtsies* – "bows".

36 *Though our silence . . . cars* – "Even if our silence must be dragged from us with great difficulty"; *cars* must mean "horses and carts".
37 *an austere regard of control* – "a severe look of authority".
38 *take you . . . lips* – "give you a blow on the mouth".
39 *scab* – another term of abuse.

FABIAN

O, peace, peace, peace! Now, now.   50

MALVOLIO

Seven of my people, with an obedient start, make out[33] for
him. I frown the while, and perchance wind up my watch, or
play with my –[34] some rich jewel. Toby approaches, curtsies[35]
there to me, –

SIR TOBY

Shall this fellow live?   55

FABIAN

Though our silence be drawn from us with cars,[36] yet peace!

MALVOLIO

I extend my hand to him thus, quenching my familiar smile
with an austere regard of control, –[37]

SIR TOBY

And does not Toby take you a blow o' the lips[38] then?

MALVOLIO

Saying, "Cousin Toby, my fortunes, having cast me on your   60
niece, give me this prerogative of speech," –

SIR TOBY

What, what?

MALVOLIO

"You must amend your drunkenness."

SIR TOBY

Out, scab![39]

40 *warrant* – "assure".
41 The *woodcock* was taken to be a stupid bird.
42 *gin* – "trap".
43 *the spirit of humours . . . to him* – "may the spirit which controls strange characters (*humours*) suggest to him that he reads it aloud!"

44 *hand* – "handwriting".
45 *great* – "capital".
46 *in contempt of question* – "without doubt".

FABIAN

Nay, patience, or we break the sinews of our plot.   65

MALVOLIO

"Besides, you waste the treasure of your time with a foolish knight," –

SIR ANDREW

That 's me, I warrant[40] you.

MALVOLIO

"One Sir Andrew," –

SIR ANDREW

I knew 't was I; for many do call me fool.   70

MALVOLIO

[*Seeing the letter on the ground*] What employment have we here?

FABIAN

Now is the woodcock[41] near the gin.[42]

SIR TOBY

O, peace! and the spirit of humours intimate reading aloud to him![43]

MALVOLIO

[*Picking up the letter*] By my life, this is my lady's hand![44] These   75
be her very *C*'s, her *U*'s, and her *T*'s; and thus makes she her
great[45] *P*'s. It is, in contempt of question,[46] her hand.

SIR ANDREW

Her *C*'s, her *U*'s, and her *T*'s; why that?

47 *By your leave, wax* – "Give me permission (to break you), seal". Wax was used to seal letters in Shakespeare's day.

48 *Soft!* – "Well!"

49 *the impressure her Lucrece* – "the figure impressed on the wax is her (seal with a picture of) Lucretia". Lucretia, a character in a Roman story, often appeared on ladies' seals at this time.

50 *she uses to* – "it is her custom to".

51 *liver and all* – "even to his deepest passion", and not just *the palate* as compared to the liver in II.iv.94.

52 *Jove*, the chief of the gods.

53 *the number's altered* – "the metre is changed", in the following verse, which now catches his eye.

54 *brock* – "badger", an animal which was apparently thought to be boastful.

55 *a Lucrece knife* – "the knife which killed Lucretia". (See note 49 to this Scene.)

56 *M, O, A, I.* All these letters occur in Malvolio's name, and, although many suggestions have been made as to what they might stand for, it is probably unnecessary to go further than that.

57 *fustian* – "high sounding but stupid".

By your leave, wax[47]

MALVOLIO

[*Reading*] *To the unknown beloved, this, and my good wishes:*
Her very phrases! By your leave, wax.[47] [*He opens the letter.*]   80
Soft![48] and the impressure her Lucrece,[49] with which she uses
to[50] seal; 't is my lady. To whom should this be?

FABIAN

This wins him, liver and all.[51]

MALVOLIO

[*Reading*]   *Jove*[52] *knows I love;*
                                    But who?   85
                            Lips, do not move:
                            No man must know.

"No man must know." What follows? The number 's altered![53]
"No man must know." If this should be thee, Malvolio?

SIR TOBY

Marry, hang thee, brock![54]   90

MALVOLIO

[*Reading*]   *I may command where I adore;*
                        But silence, like a Lucrece knife,[55]
                        With bloodless stroke my heart doth gore:
                        M, O, A, I,[56] *doth sway my life.*

FABIAN

A fustian[57] riddle!   95

SIR TOBY

Excellent wench, say I.

MALVOLIO

"*M, O, A, I, doth sway my life.*" Nay, but first, let me see, let
me see, let me see.

58 *dressed him* – "got ready for him".

59 *with what . . . at it!* – "how quickly this poor hawk (*staniel*) flies out of his course (*checks*) to get it", i.e. *the dish o' poison* in the line before.

60 *formal capacity* – "normal intelligence".

61 *what should . . . portend?* – "what can this arrangement of the letters foretell?".

62 *O! ay* has the same sound as *O, I*.

63 *at a cold scent* – "at the place where the scent disappears"; as a dog follows an animal by its scent until he loses it, so Malvolio tries to track down the meaning of the letters.

64 *Sowter will . . . a fox* – "Sowter (the name of a dog) will nevertheless (*for all this*) pick it up again barking (*cry upon 't*), even though it has been as strongly scented as a fox all the time".

65 *faults* – "stops caused by losing the scent".

66 *consonancy* – "regularity".

67 *that suffers under probation* – "it fails when tested".

68 *O shall end* – "he will cry O! at the end of it all".

FABIAN

What a dish o' poison has she dressed him![58]

SIR TOBY

And with what wing the staniel checks at it![59]   100

MALVOLIO

"I may command where I adore." Why, she may command me; I serve her; she is my lady. Why, this is evident to any formal capacity;[60] there is no obstruction in this. And the end, – What should that alphabetical position portend[61]? If I could make that resemble something in me, – Softly! M, O, A. I, –   105

SIR TOBY

O! ay,[62] make up that; he is now at a cold scent.[63]

FABIAN

Sowter will cry upon 't, for all this, though it be as rank as a fox.[64]

MALVOLIO

M, Malvolio; M, why, that begins my name!

FABIAN

Did not I say he would work it out? the cur is excellent at   110
faults.[65]

MALVOLIO

M, – but then there is no consonancy[66] in the sequel; that suffers under probation;[67] A should follow, but O does.

FABIAN

And O shall end,[68] I hope.

SIR TOBY

Ay, or I 'll cudgel him, and make him cry O!   115

111

69 *behind* – "at the end".

70 *an you* – "and if *you*".

71 *at your heels* – "behind you".

72 *this simulation . . . former* – "this problem is not (as easy) as the one before", i.e. the first part of the letter: *I may command where I adore*, which clearly referred to him.

73 *to crush this . . . me* – "if I forced the meaning of this part a little, it would apply to me".

74 *revolve* – "consider".

75 *In my stars* – "According to my fortune", as thought to be controlled by the position of the stars at a person's birth.

76 *Thy Fates.* The Fates are described in classical literature as three sisters who control human lives; one spins the thread of life, another guides it, and the third cuts it.

77 *thy blood* – "your courage".

78 *embrace them* – "take them (i.e. your Fates, and the fortunes they have to offer) willingly".

79 *like* – "likely".

80 *Be opposite* – "Disagree".

81 *tang* – "sound out".

82 *arguments of state* – "important government matters".

83 *put thyself . . . singularity* – "assume unusual habits".

84 *Remember who . . . cross-gartered.* It seems that Malvolio occasionally wore yellow stockings and strips of cloth tied cross-ways round his leg (he was *cross-gartered*). Maria here deceives him into thinking that this is a fashion which Olivia likes; she says later (lines 169–71) that Olivia in fact hates it.

85 *alter services* – "change positions", i.e. make Malvolio master of her house.

86 THE FORTUNATE-UNHAPPY – "The one who is of good fortune (i.e. rich), but unhappy (in love)".

87 *Daylight . . . more* – "Daylight and open country could not make it plainer".

88 *open* – "quite clear".

89 *politic authors* – "authors who write on politics".

90 *gross acquaintance* – "common friendships".

91 *point-devise* – "down to the smallest detail".

92 *jade me* – "make a fool of me".

93 *She did commend . . .* Malvolio seems to have taken this commendation from the letter, since, as Maria knew, Olivia really hated the fashion.

94 *of late* – "recently".

MALVOLIO

And then *I* comes behind.[69]

FABIAN

Ay, an you[70] had any eye behind you, you might see more detraction at your heels[71] than fortunes before you.

MALVOLIO

M, O, A, I; this simulation is not as the former;[72] and yet, to crush this a little, it would bow to me,[73] for every one of these 120 letters are in my name. Soft! here follows prose.
[*Reading*] *If this fall into thy hand, revolve!*[74] *In my stars*[75] *I am above thee; but be not afraid of greatness; some are born great, some achieve greatness, and some have greatness thrust upon them. Thy Fates*[76] *open their hands; let thy blood*[77] *and spirit embrace them,*[78] *and to inure thyself to what thou art like*[79] *to be, cast thy humble slough and appear fresh. Be opposite*[80] *with a kinsman, surly with servants; let thy tongue tang*[81] *arguments of state;*[82] *put thyself into the trick of singularity:*[83] *she thus advises thee that sighs for thee. Remember who commended thy yellow stockings, and wished to see thee ever cross-gartered;*[84] *I say, remember. Go to, thou art made if thou desirest to be so; if not, let me see thee a steward still, the fellow of servants, and not worthy to touch Fortune's fingers. Farewell. She that would alter services*[85] *with thee,*

THE FORTUNATE-UNHAPPY[86]

Daylight and champain discovers not more;[87] this is open.[88] 135
I will be proud, I will read politic authors,[89] I will baffle Sir Toby,
I will wash off gross acquaintance,[90] I will be point-devise[91] the
very man. I do not now fool myself, to let imagination jade
me;[92] for every reason excites to this, that my lady loves me.
She did commend[93] my yellow stockings of late;[94] she did 140
praise my leg being cross-gartered; and in this she manifests herself to my love, and with a kind of injunction drives me to these
habits of her liking. I thank my stars I am happy. I will be

95 *strange* – "distant, unfriendly".
96 *stout* – "lordly".
97 *Jove*; see note 52 above.
98 *smiling*; up to now Malvolio has appeared solemn and formal.
99 *that thou wilt have me* – "that you want me (to do)".

100 *from the Sophy* – "by the Shah (of Persia)"; Shakespeare may have heard of an Englishman, Sir Robert Shirley, who had returned with a great reward from the Shah at about the time this play was written.
101 *gull-catcher* – "one who catches fools".

114

strange,[95] stout,[96] in yellow stockings, and cross-gartered, even
with the swiftness of putting on. Jove[97] and my stars be praised! 145
Here is yet a postscript.

[*Reading*] *Thou canst not choose but know who I am. If thou enter-*
tainest my love, let it appear in thy smiling;[98] thy smile becomes thee
well; therefore in my presence still smile, dear my sweet, I prithee.

Jove, I thank thee. I will smile; I will do every thing that thou 150
wilt have me.[99]

[*Exit*

FABIAN

I will not give my part of this sport for a pension of thousands
to be paid from the Sophy.[100]

SIR TOBY

I could marry this wench for this device.

SIR ANDREW

So could I too.   155

SIR TOBY

And ask no other dowry with her but such another jest.

SIR ANDREW

Nor I neither.

FABIAN

Here comes my noble gull-catcher.[101]

Re-enter MARIA

SIR TOBY

Wilt thou set thy foot o' my neck?

SIR ANDREW

Or o' mine either?   160

115

102 *play . . . tray-trip* – "play 'tray-
trip' (a card game) with you for
my freedom", and, it seems, lose
the game and his freedom, thus
becoming her husband (*bond-
slave*).

103 *must* – "will certainly".

104 *aqua-vitae* – a strong drink; mid-
wives were said to be particularly
fond of it.

105 *addicted to a melancholy* – "disposed
to sadness", since she has recently
lost a brother.

106 *turn him . . . contempt* – "make
him particularly disagreeable to
her".

107 *Tartar* – "Tartarus", the place of
spirits in the lower world after
death.

SIR TOBY

Shall I play my freedom at tray-trip,[102] and become thy bond-slave?

SIR ANDREW

I' faith, or I either?

SIR TOBY

Why, thou hast put him in such a dream, that when the image
of it leaves him he must[103] run mad.   165

MARIA

Nay, but say true; does it work upon him?

SIR TOBY

Like aqua-vitae[104] with a midwife.

MARIA

If you will then see the fruits of the sport, mark his first approach before my lady; he will come to her in yellow stockings, and 't is a colour she abhors; and cross-gartered, a fashion 170
she detests; and he will smile upon her, which will now be so
unsuitable to her disposition, being addicted to a melancholy[105]
as she is, that it cannot but turn him into a notable contempt.[106]
If you will see it, follow me.

SIR TOBY

To the gates of Tartar,[107] thou most excellent devil of wit.   175

SIR ANDREW

I 'll make one too.

[Exeunt

(III.i) Viola is again at Olivia's house, and meets the people who are staying there. When Olivia and Maria come in, Olivia quickly dismisses the rest, and, left alone with "Cesario", she openly declares her love.

1 *tabor* – a small drum.

2 *Save thee* – "May God save thee".

3 *live by thy tabor* – "make a living by playing the tabor". But Feste pretends to misunderstand, and takes *by* to mean "by the side of"; Viola in turn misunderstands him, taking him to be a priest (*churchman*) since he lives by the church.

4 *lies* – "lives".

5 *You have said* – "You are quite right".

6 *a cheveril glove* – a glove made of the skin of a kid, which is soft and can be stretched and turned inside out very easily. The *good wit* can turn a sentence about at will.

7 *they that dally ... wanton* – "those who play cleverly (*dally nicely*) with words can easily give them double meanings", i.e. make their meanings loose (*wanton*).

Dost thou live by thy tabor[3]

118

ACT THREE

Scene I. Olivia's Garden.
Enter VIOLA *and* FESTE *with a tabor.*[1]

VIOLA

Save thee,[2] friend, and thy music. Dost thou live by thy tabor?[3]

FESTE

No, sir, I live by the church.

VIOLA

Art thou a churchman?

FESTE

No such matter, sir; I do live by the church, for I do live at my
house, and my house doth stand by the church.   5

VIOLA

So thou mayest say, the king lies[4] by a beggar if a beggar dwell
near him; or, the church stands by thy tabor, if thy tabor stand
by the church.

FESTE

You have said,[5] sir. To see this age! A sentence is but a cheveril
glove[6] to a good wit; how quickly the wrong side may be   10
turned outward!

VIOLA

Nay, that 's certain; they that dally nicely with words may
quickly make them wanton.[7]

FESTE

I would therefore my sister had had no name, sir.

119

8 *words are ... them* – "words have become rascals since people began trying to fix their meanings". He probably means that as soon as people began "putting words into *bonds*", i.e. fixing them, the words disliked it and did all they could to break away. This makes it easy for them to be given double meanings.

9 *yield* – "give".
10 *I am loath ... them* – "I am unwilling (*loath*) to use them in proving what I say to be reasonable".
11 *fool* – "clown".
12 *folly* – the amusement provided by a clown.

VIOLA

Why, man?   15

FESTE

Why, sir, her name 's a word; and to dally with that word might
make my sister wanton. But indeed words are very rascals since
bonds disgraced them.[8]

VIOLA

Thy reason, man?

FESTE

Troth, sir, I can yield[9] you none without words; and words   20
are grown so false, I am loath to prove reason with them.[10]

VIOLA

I warrant thou art a merry fellow, and carest for nothing.

FESTE

Not so, sir; I do care for something; but in my conscience, sir,
I do not care for you; if that be to care for nothing, sir, I would
it would make you invisible.   25

VIOLA

Art not thou the Lady Olivia's fool?[11]

FESTE

No, indeed, sir; the Lady Olivia has no folly;[12] she will keep
no fool, sir, till she be married; and fools are as like husbands
as pilchards are to herrings – the husband 's the bigger. I am indeed not her fool, but her corrupter of words.   30

121

13 *late* – "recently".

14 *the orb* – "the earth".

15 *I would . . . with* – "I should be sorry, sir, if the fool were not as often with . . ."; *but* – "if . . . not".

16 *your wisdom* – "your wise self".

17 *pass upon me* – "make fun of me".

18 *I 'll no more* – "I 'll stay no longer".

19 *expenses for thee* – "something for you to spend".

20 *in his next commodity of hair* – "the next time he sends a quantity of hair (to human beings)". Viola, although disguised as a man, is not wearing a beard, and Feste makes fun of her over this. She says (lines 39–40) she is almost sick for one, but she is thinking of Orsino's.

21 *within* – "indoors, at home".

22 *have bred* – "have had children".

23 *play Lord Pandarus . . . Troilus.* In an old story Troilus employs Pandarus to bring him to Cressida, the woman with whom he is secretly in love.

VIOLA

I saw thee late[13] at the Count Orsino's.

FESTE

Foolery, sir, does walk about the orb[14] like the sun; it shines everywhere. I would be sorry, sir, but the fool should be as oft with[15] your master as with my mistress. I think I saw your wisdom[16] there. 35

VIOLA

Nay, an thou pass upon me,[17] I 'll no more[18] with thee. Hold, there 's expenses for thee.[19]

[*Gives him a piece of money*

FESTE

Now Jove, in his next commodity of hair,[20] send thee a beard!

VIOLA

By my troth, I 'll tell thee, I am almost sick for one, though I would not have it grow on *my* chin. Is thy lady within?[21] 40

FESTE

[*Looking at the money*] Would not a pair of these have bred,[22] sir?

VIOLA

Yes, being kept together and put to use.

FESTE

I would play Lord Pandarus of Phrygia, sir, to bring a Cressida to this Troilus.[23] 45

24 *begging but a beggar* – "since I only beg on behalf of someone who was herself a beggar". Cressida was in the end reduced to poverty.

25 *construe* – "explain".

26 *them* – "her and her household".

27 *would* – "want".

28 *welkin* – "sky", and extended by Feste to mean "region, proper sphere"; but the word cannot really mean that, and he goes on to explain why he so used it.

29 *to play the fool* – "to work as a professional fool", which, although it sounds simple, needs some wisdom, as Viola explains.

30 *wit* – "cleverness", as well as the ordinary wit which a fool must speak with.

31 *He must observe . . . time* – "he must have regard to the humour of the people he is going to joke with, their rank (*The quality of persons*), and the occasion".

32 *Not, like . . . his eye* – "and not, like an untrained hawk (*haggard*), fly at every bird it sees"; the clown must not take up any matter which presents itself, whether suitable or not. (For *check* used in this sense, see II.v.100.)

33 *a wise man's art* – "the work of a wise man". Notice how *wise* and *wisely* in this speech contrast with *fool* and *folly*.

34 *For folly . . . wit* – "The fooling that he enacts wisely suits (the situation); but wise men, when they stoop to folly (*folly-fall'n*, "fallen into folly"), completely spoil their reputation for wisdom."

35 *Dieu vous . . . serviteur* (French) – "God protect you, sir." "And you too; your servant". Sir Andrew apparently wants to show off his powers by using French, but when Viola replies in French he is unable to continue. All he can understand is *serviteur*.

VIOLA

I understand you, sir; 't is well begged.

FESTE

The matter, I hope, is not great, sir, begging but a beggar;[24]
Cressida was a beggar. My lady is within, sir. I will construe[25]
to them[26] whence you come; who you are and what you
would[27] are out of my welkin;[28] I might say "element", but the   50
word is overworn.

[*Exit*

VIOLA

This fellow 's wise enough to play the fool,[29]
And to do that well craves a kind of wit;[30]
He must observe their mood on whom he jests,
The quality of persons, and the time,[31]   55
Not, like the haggard, check at every feather
That comes before his eye.[32] This is a practice
As full of labour as a wise man's art,[33]
For folly that he wisely shows is fit;
But wise men, folly-fall'n, quite taint their wit.[34]   60

Enter SIR TOBY BELCH *and* SIR ANDREW AGUECHEEK

SIR TOBY

Save you, gentleman.

VIOLA

And you, sir.

SIR ANDREW

Dieu vous garde, monsieur.

VIOLA

Et vous aussi; votre serviteur.[35]

125

36 *encounter* for *enter*; Sir Toby is using a fine-sounding word – and using it incorrectly – to match Sir Andrew's French.

37 *your trade be to her* – "your business concerns her". Viola in her answer plays on the word *trade*, in the sense "commerce by sea".

38 *bound to* – "on the way to"; *bound for* (a place) is the phrase normally used of a ship.

39 *list* – "aim".

40 *Taste your legs* – "Begin to use your legs".

41 *under-stand* – "stand under".

42 *gait* – "walking", and also with play on the word *gate*.

43 *we are prevented* – "we are anticipated: something has happened to make this unnecessary" (since Olivia is coming out of the house and there is no need for Viola to enter).

44 *rare* – "fine".

45 *pregnant and vouchsafed* – "ready and graciously attentive".

126

SIR ANDREW

I hope, sir, you are; and I am yours.   65

SIR TOBY

Will you encounter[36] the house? My niece is desirous you
should enter, if your trade be to her.[37]

VIOLA

I am bound to[38] your niece, sir; I mean, she is the list[39] of my
voyage.

SIR TOBY

Taste your legs,[40] sir; put them to motion.   70

VIOLA

My legs do better under-stand[41] me, sir, than I understand what
you mean by bidding me taste my legs.

SIR TOBY

I mean, to go, sir, to enter.

VIOLA

I will answer you with gait[42] and entrance. But we are prevented.[43]   75

Enter OLIVIA *and* MARIA

[*To* OLIVIA] Most excellent accomplished lady, the heavens
rain odours on you!

SIR ANDREW

That youth 's a rare[44] courtier. "Rain odours!" – Well.

VIOLA

My matter hath no voice, lady, but to your own most pregnant
and vouchsafed[45] ear.   80

46 *I'll get . . . ready* – "I'll learn all three of them by heart, ready for use". Sir Andrew so admires these fine-sounding words that he is determined to use them himself when the occasion offers.

47 *to my hearing* – "to my meeting (with this messenger)".

48 *'T was never . . . compliment* – "The world has never been a happy place since pretending to be humble (*lowly feigning*) was considered a way of paying compliments". Olivia, remembering that Viola called herself *a gentleman* (I.v.246), a person of rank, shows surprise at hearing her now speak of herself as a servant.

49 *his must needs be* – "what is his must necessarily be".

50 *For* – "As for".

51 *Would they were* – "I wish they were".

128

SIR ANDREW

"Odours", "pregnant", and "vouchsafed"; I 'll get 'em all three all ready.[46]

OLIVIA

Let the garden door be shut, and leave me to my hearing.[47]

> [*Exeunt* SIR TOBY, SIR ANDREW, *and* MARIA

[*To* VIOLA] Give me your hand, sir.

VIOLA

My duty, madam, and most humble service.   85

OLIVIA

What is your name?

VIOLA

Cesario is your servant's name, fair princess.

OLIVIA

My servant, sir! 'T was never merry world
Since lowly feigning was called compliment.[48]
You 're servant to the Count Orsino, youth.   90

VIOLA

And he is yours, and his must needs be[49] yours;
Your servant's servant is your servant, madam.

OLIVIA

For[50] him, I think not on him; for his thoughts,
Would they were[51] blanks rather than filled with me!

VIOLA

Madam, I come to whet your gentle thoughts   95
On his behalf.

52 *to solicit* – "talk in favour of".

53 *music from the spheres.* Stars and planets moving in their spheres were believed to set up harmony unheard by human beings; this was known as "music of the spheres".

54 *After the last . . . here* – "after the enchantment you worked on me last time", when she fell in love with "Cesario".

55 *so did I abuse* – "in this way I wronged".

56 *Under your . . . sit* – "I must sit condemned by your bad opinion (*hard construction*) of me".

57 *To force* – "through forcing".

58 *none of yours* – "in no way belonged to you".

59 *what might you think?* – "what must you have thought?"

60 *Have you not* (line 108) . . . *can think?* This refers to bear-baiting (see note 4 to II.v). Her honour, like the bear, is tied to a stake and "baited" by Viola's thoughts, which are *unmuzzled*, like dogs set on the bear.

61 *receiving* – "intelligence".

62 *a cypress . . . my heart* – "(for you) my heart is not hidden by my breast, but only by a transparent black veil (*cypress*)". Viola can see into her heart as if it were covered only by the black "cypress" she is wearing.

63 *a degree to love* – "a step towards love".

64 *grize* – "step".

65 *a vulgar proof* – "a common experience".

OLIVIA

O! by your leave, I pray you,

I bade you never speak again of him;
But, would you undertake another suit,
I had rather hear you to solicit[52] that
Than music from the spheres.[53]

VIOLA

Dear lady, –   100

OLIVIA

Give me leave, beseech you. I did send,
After the last enchantment you did here,[54]
A ring in chase of you; so did I abuse[55]
Myself, my servant, and, I fear me, you;
Under your hard construction must I sit,[56]   105
To force[57] that on you, in a shameful cunning,
Which you knew none of yours,[58] what might you think?[59]
Have you not set mine honour at the stake,
And baited it with all the unmuzzled thoughts
That tyrannous heart can think?[60]   110
To one of your receiving,[61] enough is shown;
A cypress, not a bosom, hides my heart.[62]
So, let me hear you speak.

VIOLA

I pity you.

OLIVIA

That 's a degree to love.[63]

VIOLA

No, not a grize;[64] for 't is a vulgar proof[65]   115
That very oft we pity enemies.

131

66 *'t is time to smile again*, since it is useless to sigh for what cannot be given.

67 *the poor*. Olivia now seems to class "Cesario" with the low-born, and not as a gentleman. She does this in the hope that she will thus find it easier to give up her love for "him".

68 *should* – "must".

69 *proper* – "fine"; *reap* ("gather, obtain") continues the idea of *harvest* in the line before.

70 *west*, where the sun sets; Viola's time of special favour seems also to be setting.

71 *westward-ho!* – "away to the west". Boatmen on the River Thames cried "Westward-ho" and "Eastward-ho" according to which way they were ready to take passengers across the river.

72 *Grace and good disposition* – "Blessing and good health".

73 *You'll nothing* – "You do not want (to say) anything".

74 *you do think . . . are* – "you think wrongly about yourself, (that you are in love with a man)". But Olivia thinks she means, "you forget your social position".

75 *If I think . . . you* – "If so, then I think you do the same (forget *your* position)". Viola takes her to mean, "If so, then I think you are not what *you* are, either", and agrees in the following line.

76 *I am your fool* – "you make a fool of me"; and "I am fooling you" is also suggested.

OLIVIA

Why, then, methinks 't is time to smile again.[66]
O world! how apt the poor[67] are to be proud.
If one should[68] be a prey, how much the better
To fall before the lion than the wolf!   [*Clock strikes* 120
The clock upbraids me with the waste of time.
Be not afraid, good youth, I will not have you;
And yet, when wit and youth is come to harvest,
Your wife is like to reap a proper[69] man.
There lies your way, due west.[70]

VIOLA

                    Then westward-ho![71]   125
Grace and good disposition[72] attend your ladyship!
You 'll nothing,[73] madam, to my lord by me?

OLIVIA

Stay;
I prithee, tell me what thou think'st of me.

VIOLA

That you do think you are not what you are.[74]   130

OLIVIA

If I think so, I think the same of you.[75]

VIOLA

Then think you right; I am not what I am.

OLIVIA

I would you were as I would have you be!

VIOLA

Would it be better, madam, than I am?
I wish it might, for now I am your fool.[76]   135

77 *what a deal of* – "how much".
78 *A murderous guilt* – "The crime of murder".
79 *love's night is noon*, i.e. love even when hidden (as in the night) shines out as bright as noonday.
80 *maidhood* – "maidenhood".
81 *maugre* – "in spite of".
82 *Nor wit nor reason* – "neither wisdom nor caution".

83 *Do not extort* (line 144) . . . *better* – "But do not think (*extort thy reason*) from this declaration of love (*this clause*) that because it is I that woo, you must therefore refuse me; instead, bring together (*fetter*) caution and reasoning (*reason . . . with reason*) (remembering that) love is good when it is sought but better when it is given unsought".
84 *that no woman has* – "no woman has these things"; she has given her heart in love to no woman.
85 *nor never none* – "and none shall ever".

(III.ii) Sir Andrew has learnt that "Cesario" is in great favour with Olivia, and is persuaded to challenge "him" by letter to a duel. Maria tells how her letter has completely deceived Malvolio and how he has appeared dressed in a way which the letter said would please his lady.

1 *jot* – "moment".

OLIVIA

O! what a deal of[77] scorn looks beautiful
In the contempt and anger of his lip.
A murderous guilt[78] shows not itself more soon
Than love that would seem hid; love's night is noon.[79]
Cesario, by the roses of the spring,   140
By maidhood,[80] honour, truth, and every thing,
I love thee so, that, maugre[81] all thy pride,
Nor wit nor reason[82] can my passion hide.
Do not extort thy reasons from this clause,
For that I woo, thou therefore hast no cause;   145
But rather reason thus with reason fetter,
Love sought is good, but given unsought is better.[83]

VIOLA

By innocence I swear, and by my youth,
I have one heart, one bosom, and one truth,
And that no woman has;[84] nor never none[85]   150
Shall mistress be of it, save I alone.
And so adieu, good madam; never more
Will I my master's tears to you deplore.

OLIVIA

Yet come again, for thou perhaps may'st move
That heart, which now abhors, to like his love.   155
                               [*Exeunt*

Scene II. A Room in Olivia's House.

Enter SIR TOBY BELCH, SIR ANDREW AGUECHEEK, *and*
FABIAN

SIR ANDREW

No, faith, I 'll not stay a jot[1] longer.

2 *dear venom* – "my angry friend".

3 *yield* – "give".

4 *orchard* – "garden".

5 *the while* – "at the same time".

6 *argument* – "proof".

7 *'Slight*; see II.v.27 and the note to it.

8 *legitimate* – "right", as in a court of law.

9 *grand-jurymen* were jurymen who might examine a case before it went before a judge. Judgement and reason might well be said to do this, but a joke perhaps lies in the fact that a third oath, that of truth, is not mentioned by Fabian, since he is in fact deceiving Sir Andrew.

10 *since before . . . sailor* – "ever since the world began". In the first book of the Bible Noah escapes destruction in the great flood by building a boat, the ark, for himself and his family.

11 *dormouse* – "sleeping". The dormouse is a small animal which sleeps during the winter. Sir Andrew's valour is not only sleeping but very small too.

although the sheet were big enough for the bed of Ware[34] in England

SIR TOBY

Thy reason, dear venom;[2] give thy reason.

FABIAN

You must needs yield[3] your reason, Sir Andrew.

SIR ANDREW

Marry, I saw your niece do more favours to the count's
serving-man than ever she bestowed upon me; I saw 't i' the   5
orchard.[4]

SIR TOBY

Did she see thee the while,[5] old boy? Tell me that.

SIR ANDREW

As plain as I see you now.

FABIAN

This was a great argument[6] of love in her toward you.

SIR ANDREW

'Slight![7] will you make an ass o' me?   10

FABIAN

I will prove it legitimate,[8] sir, upon the oaths of judgement and
reason.

SIR TOBY

And they have been grand-jurymen[9] since before Noah was a
sailor.[10]

FABIAN

She did show favour to the youth in your sight only to exas-   15
perate you, to awake your dormouse[11] valour, to put fire in

137

12 *heart . . . liver.* These were thought to be the seats of courage as well as of love.

13 *accosted;* see note 19 to I.iii.

14 *fire-new from the mint* – "as fresh as newly-made coins".

15 *looked for at your hand* – "expected of you".

16 *this was balked* – "the opportunity for this was lost".

17 *the double . . . opportunity* – "this wonderful opportunity", golden as rich plate twice gilded.

18 *sailed into . . . opinion* – "moved to the cold side of my lady's opinion of you". Before, Sir Andrew was in the sunshine; now he is out in the cold.

19 *an icicle . . . beard.* Dutchmen were exploring the far north at the time the play was written.

20 *it,* i.e. *my lady's opinion* (line 22).

21 *policy* here means "skill in dealing with a difficult situation". But Sir Andrew misunderstands the word.

22 *I had . . . politician* – "I would as willingly (*lief*) be an over-serious churchman (*Brownist*) as a politician". By *politician* he means one who acts dishonestly for political ends. A *Brownist* was a member of the church founded by Robert Brown; Brownists took life so seriously that they were thought to be unable to laugh at a joke.

23 *me* has hardly any separate meaning in this and the following line; it implies "do it for me, to please me". Sir Toby wants Sir Andrew to think that they are both concerned in the success of Sir Andrew's courtship.

24 *shall take note* – "will certainly notice".

25 *love-broker* – "a person who arranges marriages".

26 *can* – "who can".

27 *report of valour* – "reputation for bravery".

28 *a martial hand* – "warlike handwriting", bold and firm.

29 *curst* – "sharp".

30 *it is no matter . . . so it* – "it does not matter . . . so long as it . . ."

31 *the licence of ink* – "the freedom of writing", by which one can write things one would not necessarily wish to say.

32 *thou thou'st him* – "call him 'thou'", show your contempt by addressing him as if he were a serving man (not "you", which would be the polite form of address).

33 *and . . .* The verb is *set . . . down* in line 40.

34 *the bed of Ware* is a very large bed which was once used at an inn in the town of Ware; it is big enough to hold twelve people.

35 *about it* – "get on with the work".

36 *goose-pen* – "a pen made from a goose feather". The goose was looked upon as a stupid bird, and its feathers would therefore suit Sir Andrew.

your heart, and brimstone in your liver.[12] You should then have accosted[13] her, and with some excellent jests, fire-new from the mint,[14] you should have banged the youth into dumbness. This was looked for at your hand,[15] and this was balked;[16] the   20
double gilt of this opportunity[17] you let time wash off, and you are now sailed into the north of my lady's opinion,[18] where you will hang like an icicle on a Dutchman's beard,[19] unless you do redeem it[20] by some laudable attempt, either of valour or policy.[21]   25

SIR ANDREW

An 't be any way, it must be with valour, for policy I hate; I had as lief be a Brownist as a politician.[22]

SIR TOBY

Why then, build me[23] thy fortunes upon the basis of valour; challenge me the count's youth to fight with him; hurt him in eleven places; my niece shall take note[24] of it; and assure thy-   30
self, there is no love-broker[25] in the world can[26] more prevail in man's commendation with woman than report of valour.[27]

FABIAN

There is no way but this, Sir Andrew.

SIR ANDREW

Will either of you bear me a challenge to him?

SIR TOBY

Go, write it in a martial hand;[28] be curst[29] and brief; it is no   35
matter how witty, so it[30] be eloquent and full of invention; taunt him with the licence of ink;[31] if thou thou'st[32] him some thrice, it shall not be amiss; and[33] as many lies as will lie in thy sheet of paper, although the sheet were big enough for the bed of Ware[34] in England, set 'em down; go, about it.[35] Let there   40
be gall enough in thy ink, though thou write with a goose-pen,[36] no matter; about it.

37 *cubiculo* (Latin) – "room". Sir Toby uses a Latin word to confuse Sir Andrew still further.

38 *dear manakin* – "dear little man". In the next line Sir Toby repeats *dear*, but means by it "costly". He has cost Sir Andrew a lot of money.

39 *some two thousand strong* – "a good two thousand ..." of some kind of money, perhaps dollars.

40 *then*, i.e. "if I do not".

41 *stir on ... answer* – "encourage the youth to reply".

42 *wainropes* – "cart-ropes".

43 *hale* – "pull".

44 *For* – "As for".

45 *liver*; see note 12 to this scene. A liver without blood would mean a man without courage.

46 *anatomy* – "body".

47 *opposite* – "opponent", i.e. Viola.

48 *youngest wren of nine* – (perhaps) "the dearest, smallest little bird". The earliest editions of the play all have *mine* for *nine* in this text, but *nine* is usually taken to be correct. There might be nine nestlings in a family of wrens, and the youngest would be the smallest. They have already made fun of Maria's small size (e.g. at II.iii.151).

49 *spleen* – "bad temper brought on by too much laughing".

50 *gull* – "fool".

51 *renegado* – "deserter", from his puritan view of religion.

52 *can* – "who can".

53 *impossible passages of grossness* – "unbelievably foolish actions"

And cross gartered?

*Most villainously; like a pedant⁵⁴
that keeps a school i' the church*

SIR ANDREW

Where shall I find you?

SIR TOBY

We 'll call thee at the *cubiculo*;[37] go.

[*Exit* SIR ANDREW

FABIAN

This is a dear manakin[38] to you, Sir Toby.   45

SIR TOBY

I have been dear to him, lad; some two thousand strong[39] or so.

FABIAN

We shall have a rare letter from him; but you 'll not deliver it?

SIR TOBY

Never trust me, then;[40] and by all means stir on the youth to an answer.[41] I think oxen and wainropes[42] cannot hale[43] them together. For[44] Andrew, if he were opened, and you find so much   50
blood in his liver[45] as will clog the foot of a flea, I 'll eat the rest of the anatomy.[46]

FABIAN

And his opposite,[47] the youth, bears in his visage no great presage of cruelty.

Enter MARIA

SIR TOBY

Look, where the youngest wren of nine[48] comes.   55

MARIA

If you desire the spleen,[49] and will laugh yourselves into stitches, follow me. Yond gull[50] Malvolio is turned heathen, a very renegado;[51] for there is no Christian, that means to be saved by believing rightly, can[52] ever believe such impossible passages of grossness.[53] He 's in yellow stockings!   60

141

54 *pedant* – "teacher". In Shakespeare's day it was not uncommon for a school to be kept in some part of a church.

55 *dogged him . . . murderer* – "followed him as if I were to be his murderer".

56 *the new map . . . Indies.* A new map of the East Indies had appeared at about the time *Twelfth Night* was being written. It had a great many lines on it, since it was drawn in accordance with a new system of mapping.

57 *not* – "never".

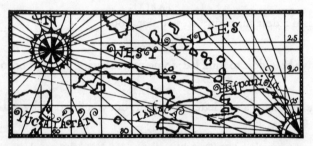

he does smile his face into more lines than is in the new map with the augmentation of the Indies[56]

(III.iii) Antonio has followed Sebastian to the town and they meet again. Antonio forces his purse on Sebastian, in case he sees anything he would like to buy.

1 SEBASTIAN *and* ANTONIO. We have already heard how Antonio rescued Sebastian after the shipwreck, and how they became friends (II.i).

2 *by my will* – "purposely".

3 *you make . . . pains* – "you enjoy giving yourself trouble".

4 *chide* – "scold".

5 *And not all . . . voyage* – "and desire to see you was not all (the cause of my following you like this), though it was as much as might have persuaded me to make a longer journey".

6 *jealousy what* – "worry as to what".

7 *Being skilless . . . parts* – "since you know nothing of these parts (of the country)".

8 *my willing love* (line 11). . . *pursuit* – "(I, persuaded by) my strong love for you, set out to follow you (*in your pursuit*) more through reasons of fear (for your safety)".

142

SIR TOBY

And cross-gartered?

MARIA

Most villainously; like a pedant[54] that keeps a school i' the church. I have dogged him like his murderer.[55] He does obey every point of the letter that I dropped to betray him; he does smile his face into more lines than is in the new map with the   65
augmentation of the Indies.[56] You have not[57] seen such a thing as 't is; I can hardly forbear hurling things at him. I know my lady will strike him; if she do, he'll smile and take 't for a great favour.

SIR TOBY

Come, bring us, bring us where he is.   70

[*Exeunt*

Scene III. A Street.
Enter SEBASTIAN *and* ANTONIO.[1]

SEBASTIAN

I would not by my will[2] have troubled you;
But since you make your pleasure of your pains,[3]
I will no further chide[4] you.

ANTONIO

I could not stay behind you; my desire,
More sharp than filéd steel, did spur me forth;   5
And not all love to see you, though so much
As might have drawn one to a longer voyage,[5]
But jealousy what[6] might befall your travel,
Being skilless in these parts,[7] which to a stranger,
Unguided and unfriended, often prove   10
Rough and unhospitable; my willing love,
The rather by these arguments of fear,
Set forth in your pursuit.[8]

143

9 *thanks; and.* These words do not appear in the earliest edition of the text, but since the line without them lacks one heavy stress it is almost certain that some words have been left out, and those suggested make good sense.

10 *oft good turns . . . pay* – "kindnesses received are often shaken off with only useless money like this (*such uncurrent pay,* i.e. the thanks just given) as a reward.

11 *were my worth . . . firm* – "if my wealth (*worth*) were as considerable (*firm*) as is my consciousness (of debt to you for your help)".

12 *You should . . . dealing* – "you would have found better business"; *dealing* continues the idea of *pay* (line 16) and *worth* (line 17).

13 *What's to do?* – "What shall we do?"

14 *relics* – "things of historical interest".

15 *'t is long to night* – "night is still a long way off, it is still quite early".

16 *renown* – "make famous".

17 *the count his* – "the count's", i.e. Orsino's.

18 *of such note* – "so considerable".

19 *it would . . . answered* – "it could hardly be defended", and his old enemies might kill him for it.

20 *Belike you slew* – "You probably killed".

21 *Albeit the quality . . . argument* – "although the seriousness of the occasion (*quality of the time*) and the quarrel might reasonably have led to killing".

22 *answered in repaying* – "completely settled by our paying back".

144

SEBASTIAN

My kind Antonio,
I can no other answer make but thanks,
And thanks, and ever thanks; and⁹ oft good turns   15
Are shuffled off with such uncurrent pay;¹⁰
But, were my worth, as is my conscience, firm,¹¹
You should find better dealing.¹² What 's to do?¹³
Shall we go see the relics¹⁴ of this town?

ANTONIO

Tomorrow, sir; best first go see your lodging.   20

SEBASTIAN

I am not weary, and 't is long to night.¹⁵
I pray you, let us satisfy our eyes
With the memorials and the things of fame
That do renown¹⁶ this city.

ANTONIO

Would you 'd pardon me;
I do not without danger walk these streets;   25
Once, in a sea-fight 'gainst the count his¹⁷ galleys,
I did some service – of such note,¹⁸ indeed,
That were I ta'en here it would scarce be answered.¹⁹

SEBASTIAN

Belike you slew²⁰ great number of his people.

ANTONIO

The offence is not of such a bloody nature,   30
Albeit the quality of the time and quarrel
Might well have given us bloody argument.²¹
It might have since been answered in repaying²²

23 *for traffic's sake* – "in the interests of trade". They settled the quarrel so that trade could begin again between them.
24 *Most of our city* – "almost everyone in our city".
25 *myself stood out* – "I myself refused (to do this)".
26 *lapséd* – "taken".
27 *the Elephant* – the name of an inn.
28 Is – "It is".

29 *bespeak our diet* – "order our food".
30 *there shall you have me* – "you will find me there".
31 *toy* – something attractive but of no great value.
32 *your store . . . markets* – "your store of money is not enough, I think, to cover the buying of things which take your fancy (but are not necessary)"; *idle* – "fanciful".

146

What we took from them; which, for traffic's sake,[23]
Most of our city[24] did; only myself stood out;[25]   35
For which, if I be lapséd[26] in this place,
I shall pay dear.

SEBASTIAN

Do not then walk too open.

ANTONIO

It doth not fit me. Hold, sir; here 's my purse.
In the south suburbs, at the Elephant,[27]
Is[28] best to lodge; I will bespeak our diet,[29]   40
Whiles you beguile the time and feed your knowledge
With viewing of the town; there shall you have me.[30]

SEBASTIAN

Why _I_ your purse?

ANTONIO

Haply your eye shall light upon some toy[31]
You have desire to purchase; and your store,   45
I think, is not for idle markets,[32] sir.

SEBASTIAN

I'll be your purse-bearer, and leave you for an hour.

ANTONIO

To the Elephant.

SEBASTIAN

I do remember.

[_Exeunt_

(III.iv) Malvolio, strangely dressed, acts before Olivia in the way which Maria's letter suggested. Olivia thinks him mad, and orders Sir Toby to take care of him. Sir Andrew has meanwhile written his challenge to "Cesario", and Sir Toby delivers it. Viola is very surprised at receiving it, for she knows of no quarrel; and then Fabian and Sir Toby pretend to Sir Andrew that Viola insists on fighting, and to Viola that Sir Andrew does. Just as they are at last brought together, Antonio comes up to them and draws his sword in defence of Viola, whom he believes to be his friend Sebastian. Sir Toby confronts him, but as they are about to fight, two of Orsino's officers enter and arrest Antonio. Before he is led away he asks Viola for his purse; but she knows nothing of it, since it was given not to her but to her twin brother Sebastian. To Sir Andrew this seems cowardly behaviour, and he is now prepared to fight "Cesario" in earnest.

1 *him*, i.e. "Cesario".
2 *he says* – "if he says". Olivia does not know for certain whether he will come or not, since the messenger she sent has not yet returned. The servant announces him in line 52.
3 *of* – "on".
4 *bought*, i.e. by gifts and feasting, not by declarations of love.

5 *sad and civil* – "serious and formal".
6 *suits well . . . fortunes* – "is behaving in a way which suits a servant (to a mistress) in my condition".
7 *possessed* – "possessed by the devil; mad".
8 *your ladyship were best* – "it would be best for your ladyship".

148

Scene IV. Olivia's Garden.
Enter OLIVIA *and* MARIA.

OLIVIA

I have sent after him;[1] he says[2] he 'll come,
How shall I feast him, what bestow of[3] him?
For youth is bought[4] more oft than begged or borrowed.
I speak too loud.
Where is Malvolio? He is sad and civil,[5]   5
And suits well for a servant with my fortunes;[6]
Where is Malvolio?

MARIA

He 's coming, madam; but in very strange manner. He is, sure,
possessed,[7] madam.

OLIVIA

Why, what 's the matter? Does he rave?   10

MARIA

No, madam; he does nothing but smile; your ladyship were
best[8] to have some guard about you if he come, for sure the man
is tainted in 's wits.

OLIVIA

Go call him hither.   [*Exit* MARIA
I am as mad as he,   15
If sad and merry madness equal be.

Re-enter MARIA *with* MALVOLIO

How now, Malvolio!

MALVOLIO

Sweet lady, ho, ho.

149

9 *sonnet* – "poem", which contains this proverbial line.

10 *how dost thou* – "how are you".

11 *Roman hand* – "handwriting in the Italian style".

12 *At* your *request!* – "Must I answer you (a serving-girl)!"

13 *nightingales answer daws* – "nightingales (birds with a sweet song) seem to sing in answer to the call of jackdaws (which make an ugly noise)" – so he may as well answer her.

perferretur. Id quod nos facimus, ut vos vocemus, non solum ad nostri gaudij participationem, Verum etiam ad piarum precum communionem, quas DEO, Vna nobiscum, pro hoc beneficio, tam optato nobis, tam expectato uiris ommibus Amiis, libenter (non dubitamus) facietis. DEVS V. E. diu seruet incolumem. Ex Regia ura, Hamptomæ

ur⁰   D⁰   L⁰   V⁰

I think we do know the sweet Roman hand¹¹

OLIVIA

Smilest thou?
I sent for thee upon a sad occasion.   20

MALVOLIO

Sad, lady! I could be sad; this does make some obstruction in
the blood, this cross-gartering; but what of that? If it please the
eye of one, it is with me as the very true sonnet[9] is, "Please one,
and please all".

OLIVIA

Why, how dost thou,[10] man? What is the matter with thee?   25

MALVOLIO

Not black in my mind, though yellow in my legs. It did come
to his hands, and commands shall be executed; I think we do
know the sweet Roman hand.[11]

OLIVIA

Wilt thou go to bed, Malvolio?

MALVOLIO

To bed! ay, sweetheart, and I 'll come to thee.   30

OLIVIA

God comfort thee! Why dost thou smile so, and kiss thy hand
so oft?

MARIA

How do you, Malvolio?

MALVOLIO

At your request![12] Yes; nightingales answer daws.[13]

MARIA

Why appear you with this ridiculous boldness before my lady?   35

151

14 *writ* for *written*.

MALVOLIO

"Be not afraid of greatness"; 't was well writ.[14]

OLIVIA

What meanest thou by that, Malvolio?

MALVOLIO

"Some are born great," –

OLIVIA

Ha!

MALVOLIO

"Some achieve greatness," –   40

OLIVIA

What sayest thou?

MALVOLIO

"And some have greatness thrust upon them."

OLIVIA

Heaven restore thee!

MALVOLIO

"Remember who commended thy yellow stockings," –

OLIVIA

Thy yellow stockings!   45

MALVOLIO

"And wished to see thee cross-gartered."

OLIVIA

Cross-gartered!

15 *very midsummer madness* – "the worst of all madness", supposedly brought on by the heat of mid-summer.

16 *miscarry* – "come to harm".

17 *do you . . . now* – "are you beginning to understand me now?" Malvolio is addressing Olivia, who, before she left, gave orders that her uncle Sir Toby should look after him. But in fact, of course, she understood nothing of what Malvolio said to her.

18 *consequently* – "then".

MALVOLIO

"Go to, thou art made, if thou desirest to be so;" –

OLIVIA

Am I made?

MALVOLIO

"If not, let me see thee a servant still."   50

OLIVIA

Why, this is very midsummer madness.[15]

Enter Servant

SERVANT

Madam, the young gentleman of the Count Orsino's is returned. I could hardly entreat him back; he attends your ladyship's pleasure.

OLIVIA

I 'll come to him.   55

                              [*Exit* Servant

Good Maria, let this fellow be looked to. Where 's my cousin Toby? Let some of my people have a special care of him; I would not have him miscarry[16] for the half of my dowry.

                              [*Exeunt* OLIVIA *and* MARIA

MALVOLIO

O, ho! do you come near me now?[17] No worse man than Sir Toby to look to me! This concurs directly with the letter; she   60 sends him on purpose that I may appear stubborn to him; for she incites me to that in the letter. "Cast thy humble slough," says she; "be opposite with a kinsman, surly with servants; let thy tongue tang with arguments of state; put thyself into the trick of singularity"; and consequently[18] sets down the manner   65

155

19 *carriage* – "way of moving".
20 *in the habit . . . note* – "in the dress of some important person", perhaps a particular person known to the audience who wore yellow stockings and cross-gartering.
21 *limed* – "caught" (see Glossary under *lime*).
22 *fellow*. Malvolio takes fellow to mean "friend (of mine)", even though this meaning of the word was probably disappearing by the time Shakespeare wrote, and it was more frequently used in addressing servants.
23 *after my degree* – "according to my rank".

24 *scruple* means (a) a very small weight and (b) "doubt". A *dram* is also a weight, three times that of a scruple. Malvolio plays on the two meanings of *scruple*.
25 *incredulous* – "doubtful".
26 *in little* – "to a small scale".
27 *Legion* – "a great number (of devils)". In the Bible Jesus asks a man possessed by evil spirits what his name is. He answers, "My name is Legion, for we (i.e. the spirits) are many" (Mark v. 9).
28 *private* – "privacy".
29 *hollow* – "deep-voiced". Evil spirits were supposed to speak in this way.

156

how; as, a sad face, a reverend carriage,[19] a slow tongue, in the habit of some sir of note,[20] and so forth. I have limed[21] her; but it is Jove's doing, and Jove make me thankful! And when she went away now, "Let this fellow be looked to"; fellow![22] not Malvolio, nor after my degree,[23] but fellow. Why, every- 70 thing adheres together, that no dram of a scruple,[24] no scruple of a scruple, no obstacle, no incredulous[25] or unsafe circumstance – What can be said? Nothing that can be can come between me and the full prospect of my hopes. Well, Jove, not I, is the doer of this, and he is to be thanked. 75

Re-enter MARIA, *with* SIR TOBY BELCH *and* FABIAN

SIR TOBY

Which way is he, in the name of sanctity? If all the devils of hell be drawn in little,[26] and Legion[27] himself possessed him, yet I 'll speak to him.

FABIAN

Here he is, here he is. [*To* MALVOLIO] How is 't with you, sir?

SIR TOBY

How is 't with you, man? 80

MALVOLIO

Go off; I discard you; let me enjoy my private;[28] go off.

MARIA

Lo, how hollow[29] the fiend speaks within him! Did not I tell you? Sir Toby, my lady prays you to have a care of him.

MALVOLIO

Ah ha! does she so?

157

30 *let me alone.* Sir Toby is telling
Maria and Fabian not to interfere
with him while he is looking after
Malvolio.
31 *La you.* This was a phrase used to
call the hearer's attention to something important; "Look!"

32 *wise woman* – "woman supposed
to be able to cure sick people".
33 *move* – "anger".
34 *rough* – "violent".
35 *used* – "treated".

SIR TOBY

Go to, go to; peace! peace! We must deal gently with him; 85
let me alone.[30] How do you, Malvolio? How is 't with you?
What, man! defy the devil; consider, he 's an enemy to mankind.

MALVOLIO

Do you know what you say?

MARIA

[*To* SIR TOBY *and* FABIAN] La you![31] an you speak ill of the 90
devil, how he takes it at heart. Pray God, he be not be-
witched!

FABIAN

Carry his water to the wise woman.[32]

MARIA

Marry, and it shall be done tomorrow morning if I live. My
lady would not lose him for more than I 'll say. 95

MALVOLIO

How now, mistress!

MARIA

O Lord!

SIR TOBY

Prithee, hold thy peace; this is not the way; do you not see you
move[33] him? Let me alone with him.

FABIAN

No way but gentleness; gently, gently; the fiend is rough,[34] 100
and will not be roughly used.[35]

36 *bawcock* – "fine fellow", or, more literally, "fine bird".

37 *chuck* is a form of *chick*, and also means "fellow".

38 *Biddy* is a child's name for chicken, and thus continues the idea of comparing Malvolio to a bird, as in *bawcock* and *chuck* above. *Ay, Biddy, come with me* may be part of an old song.

39 *'t is not . . . Satan* – "it is not proper for a person of your seriousness (*gravity*) to play games with Satan (i.e. be on friendly terms with him)". Cherry-pit was played by throwing cherry-stones into a small hole.

40 *foul collier* – "devil", as being like a miner (*collier*), since both were black and the devil, like the miner, was thought to work beneath the ground.

41 *element* – "world".

42 *could* – "should".

43 *His very genius . . . device* – "His very soul has been affected by the plot".

44 *lest the device . . . taint* – "in case the plot becomes known and spoilt"; the phrase probably continues the idea of *infection* in line 114: food infected by bad air becomes tainted, i.e. spoilt.

SIR TOBY

Why, how now, my bawcock![36] how dost thou, chuck?[37]

MALVOLIO

Sir!

SIR TOBY

Ay, Biddy,[38] come with me. What, man! 't is not for gravity
to play at cherry-pit with Satan;[39] hang him, foul collier![40]   105

MARIA

Get him to say his prayers, good Sir Toby; get him to pray.

MALVOLIO

My prayers, minx!

MARIA

No, I warrant you, he will not hear of godliness.

MALVOLIO

Go, hang yourselves all! You are idle, shallow things; I am not
of your element.[41] You shall know more hereafter.   110
                                                                    [*Exit*

SIR TOBY

Is 't possible?

FABIAN

If this were played upon a stage now, I could[42] condemn it as an
improbable fiction.

SIR TOBY

His very genius hath taken the infection of the device,[43] man.

MARIA

Nay, pursue him now, lest the device take air, and taint.[44]   115

45 *in a dark ... bound.* In Shakespeare's day it was thought that
madness could best be treated by
having the patient tied up (*bound*),
and put into a dark room.

46 *carry* – "manage".

47 *bring ... to the bar* – "make ...
known to everybody".

48 *crown thee ... madmen* – "make
you king of those who expose
madmen".

49 *a May morning*; May was a month
associated with merry-making.

50 *vinegar and pepper*; vinegar is sharp
to the taste, and pepper hot.
Fabian, in the next line, plays on
the idea by using *saucy* to mean (*a*)
"with sauce in it" and (*b*) "rude".

162

FABIAN

Why, we shall make him mad indeed.

MARIA

The house will be the quieter.

SIR TOBY

Come, we'll have him in a dark room, and bound.[45] My niece is already in the belief that he's mad; we may carry[46] it thus, for our pleasure and his penance, till our very pastime, tired out of 120 breath, prompt us to have mercy on him; at which time we will bring the device to the bar,[47] and crown thee for a finder of madmen.[48] But see, but see.

Enter SIR ANDREW AGUECHEEK

FABIAN

More matter for a May morning.[49]

SIR ANDREW

Here's the challenge; read it; I warrant there's vinegar and 125 pepper[50] in 't.

FABIAN

Is 't so saucy?

SIR ANDREW

Ay, is 't, I warrant him; do but read.

SIR TOBY

Give me. [*Takes the letter and reads*] *Youth, whatsoever thou art, thou art but a scurvy fellow.* 130

FABIAN

Good and valiant.

51 *admire not* – "do not be surprised".
52 *A good . . . law* – "A good remark, one which will save you from trouble with the law". No legal action can be taken against Sir Andrew, since he accuses the "youth" of nothing.
53 *uses thee* – 'treats you'.
54 *thou liest in thy throat* – "you lie completely".
55 *sense-less*; the last part is said so that Sir Andrew cannot hear.

56 *o' the windy . . . law* – "on the safe side of the law", because, it seems, he compares his opponent to a rogue and a villain, but does not actually call him by these names.
57 *He may . . . better.* He is speaking of the possibility of one of them being killed; *he* may be the one to die, but his hope is better, i.e. that his opponent will die instead.
58 *thou usest* – "you treat".

164

SIR TOBY

*Wonder not, nor admire not[51] in thy mind, why I do call thee so, for
I will show thee no reason for 't.*

FABIAN

A good note, that keeps you from the blow of the law.[52]

SIR TOBY

Thou comest to the Lady Olivia, and in my sight she uses thee[53] 135
*kindly; but thou liest in thy throat;[54] that is not the matter I challenge
thee for.*

FABIAN

Very brief, and to exceeding good sense-less.[55]

SIR TOBY

I will waylay thee going home; where, if it be thy chance to kill me, –

FABIAN

Good.   140

SIR TOBY

Thou killest me like a rogue and a villain.

FABIAN

Still you keep o' the windy side of the law;[56] good.

SIR TOBY

*Fare thee well; and God have mercy upon one of our souls! He may
have mercy upon mine, but my hope is better;[57] and so look to thyself. Thy friend, as thou usest[58] him, and thy sworn enemy.*   145
                              ANDREW AGUECHEEK
If this letter move him not, his legs cannot. I 'll give 't him.

165

59 *fit occasion* – "suitable opportunity".
60 *commerce* – "conversation".
61 *scout me for him* – "help me by watching for him".
62 *a bum-baily* was a bailiff, a court officer who went out to arrest debtors and those who were not carrying out court orders.
63 *draw* – "pull out your sword".
64 *sharply twanged off* – "said in a loud, self-assured way".
65 *gives manhood . . . itself* – "gives a man greater reputation for courage (*approbation*) than actual testing (*proof*)".

66 *gives him out* – "shows him".
67 *clodpole* – "fool".
68 *set upon . . . valour* – "give Aguecheek a particular reputation for bravery".
69 *cockatrices* – imaginary animals supposed to be able to kill their prey simply by looking at it.
70 *give them . . . leave* – "make way for them until he leaves".
71 *presently* – "at once".

MARIA

You may have very fit occasion[59] for 't; he is now in some commerce[60] with my lady, and will by and by depart.

SIR TOBY

Go, Sir Andrew; scout me for him[61] at the corner of the orchard, like a bum-baily;[62] so soon as ever thou seest him,   150
draw;[63] and, as thou drawest, swear horrible; for it comes to pass oft that a terrible oath, with a swaggering accent sharply twanged off,[64] gives manhood more approbation than ever proof itself[65] would have earned him. Away!

SIR ANDREW

Nay, let me alone for swearing.   155

[*Exit*

SIR TOBY

Now will not I deliver his letter; for the behaviour of the young gentleman gives him out[66] to be of good capacity and breeding; his employment between his lord and my niece con-firms no less; therefore this letter, being so excellently ignorant, will breed no terror in the youth; he will find it comes from a   160
clodpole.[67] But, sir, I will deliver his challenge by word of mouth; set upon Aguecheek a notable report of valour;[68] and drive the gentleman, as I know his youth will aptly receive it, into a most hideous opinion of his rage, skill, fury, and im-petuosity. This will so fright them both that they will kill one   165
another by the look, like cockatrices.[69]

FABIAN

Here he comes with your niece; give them way till he take leave,[70] and presently[71] after him.

SIR TOBY

I will meditate the while upon some horrid message for a chal-lenge.   170

[*Exeunt* SIR TOBY, FABIAN, *and* MARIA

72 *laid mine honour . . . on 't* – "expended my reputation too abundantly (*unchary*) on it (this declaration of love)".

73 *'haviour* for *behaviour* – "character".

74 *this jewel* is a small portrait of Olivia set with precious stones.

75 *What shall you . . . give?* – "What will you ask me for, and I refuse, that I may give you honourably for the asking?"; there is nothing she will refuse Viola if it can be done honourably.

76 *acquit you* – "free you (from your promise)".

wear this jewel[74] *for me; 't is my picture*

Re-enter OLIVIA, *with* VIOLA

OLIVIA

I have said too much unto a heart of stone,
And laid mine honour too unchary on 't;[72]
There 's something in me that reproves my fault,
But such a headstrong potent fault it is
That it but mocks reproof.   175

VIOLA

With the same 'haviour[73] that your passion bears,
Goes on my master's grief.

OLIVIA

Here; wear this jewel[74] for me; 't is my picture;
Refuse it not; it hath no tongue to vex you;
And I beseech you come again tomorrow.   180
What shall you ask of me that I 'll deny,
That honour saved may upon asking give?[75]

VIOLA

Nothing but this: your true love for my master.

OLIVIA

How with mine honour may I give him that
Which I have given to you?

VIOLA

                    I will acquit you.[76]   185

OIIVIA

Well, come again tomorrow; fare you well;
A fiend like thee might bear my soul to hell.

[*Exit*

77 *That defence . . . to 't* – "whatever defence you have, take yourself to it".

78 *are thou* – "are that thou".

79 *despite* – "anger".

80 *bloody as the hunter* – "as blood-thirsty as the hunting-dog".

81 *attends* – "waits for".

82 *Dismount thy tuck* – "Draw your sword".

83 *be yare . . . preparation* – "get ready quickly".

84 *to* – "with".

85 *opposite* – "opponent".

86 *withal* – "with".

87 *dubbed with . . . consideration* – "given knighthood (*dubbed*) with a sword unmarked from war (*unhatched*) and kneeling on a carpet (not on the field of battle)". The king or queen touched a man on the shoulder with a sword when giving him knighthood, often as a reward for courage in war; but Sir Andrew's honour has nothing military about it.

88 *souls and bodies . . . three* – "he has separated three souls from their bodies", i.e. killed three people.

89 *incensement* – "anger".

90 *satisfaction can be none* – "there can be no satisfying him".

91 *Hob, nob* – "Come what may". Whatever the risk, he will fight.

SCENE IV]

Re-enter SIR TOBY BELCH *and* FABIAN

SIR TOBY

Gentleman, God save thee.

VIOLA

And you, sir.

SIR TOBY

That defence thou hast, betake thee to 't;[77] of what nature the 190
wrongs are thou[78] hast done him, I know not; but thy inter-
cepter, full of despite,[79] bloody as the hunter,[80] attends[81] thee at
the orchard-end. Dismount thy tuck,[82] be yare in thy preparation,[83] for thy assailant is quick, skilful, and deadly.

VIOLA

You mistake, sir; I am sure no man hath any quarrel to[84] me; 195
my remembrance is very free and clear from any image of
offence done to any man.

SIR TOBY

You 'll find it otherwise, I assure you; therefore, if you hold
your life at any price, betake you to your guard; for your opposite[85] hath in him what youth, strength, skill, and wrath can 200
furnish man withal.[86]

VIOLA

I pray you, sir, what is he?

SIR TOBY

He is knight, dubbed with unhatched rapier, and on carpet
consideration;[87] but he is a devil in private brawl; souls and
bodies hath he divorced three,[88] and his incensement[89] at this 205
moment is so implacable that satisfaction can be none[90] but by
pangs of death and sepulchre. Hob, nob,[91] is his word; give 't
or take 't.

171

92 *desire some . . . lady* – "ask the lady of the house for someone to protect me".
93 *taste* – "test".
94 *belike* – "perhaps".
95 *quirk* – "strange character".
96 *derives itself . . . injury* – "comes from a very sufficient insult".
97 *that*, i.e. to meet and fight.

98 *meddle* – "become concerned in this affair".
99 *iron*, i.e. a sword.
100 *as to know of* – "to find out from".
101 *something of . . . purpose* – "something arising from my negligence, and not done on purpose".
102 *to a mortal arbitrement* – "to decision by fighting to the death".

VIOLA

I will return again into the house, and desire some conduct of the lady,[92] I am no fighter. I have heard of some kind of men 210 that put quarrels purposely on others to taste[93] their valour; belike[94] this is a man of that quirk.[95]

SIR TOBY

Sir, no; his indignation derives itself out of a very competent injury![96] Therefore get you on and give him his desire. Back you shall not to the house, unless you undertake that[97] with me 215 which with as much safety you might answer him; therefore on, or strip your sword stark naked; for meddle[98] you must, that 's certain, or forswear to wear iron[99] about you.

VIOLA

This is as uncivil as strange. I beseech you, do me this courteous office, as to know of[100] the knight what my offence to 220 him is; it is something of my negligence, nothing of my purpose.[101]

SIR TOBY

I will do so. Signior Fabian, stay you by this gentleman till my return.

[*Exit*

VIOLA

Pray you, sir, do you know of this matter? 225

FABIAN

I know the knight is incensed against you, even to a mortal arbitrement,[102] but nothing of the circumstance more.

VIOLA

I beseech you, what manner of man is he?

173

103 *to read him by his form* – "to judge by his appearance".

104 *like* – "likely".

105 *much bound* – "very grateful".

106 *sir priest . . . sir knight.* Priests were addressed as *sir* because they had normally taken an academic degree; knights, too, were spoken of as *sir*. Viola thus brings two uses of *sir* together.

107 *Exeunt.* In the modern theatre a change of scene would take place here. On the stage of Shakespeare's time, however, it would have been possible for the two groups, Fabian and Viola, on the one hand, and Sir Toby and Sir Andrew, on the other, to withdraw in turn as required by the plot.

108 *firago* is probably Sir Toby's mistake for *virago*, "a warlike woman"; it is significant of Sir Toby's doubts as to Viola's bravery that he calls her by a name normally applied to a woman.

109 *pass* – "a round (of fencing)".

110 *he gives me the stuck-in* – "he gave me the thrust". Sir Toby uses the present tense (*gives* for *gave*) to make his story more immediate and convincing.

111 *with such . . . inevitable* – "with such a deadly blow that I could not escape it (*it is inevitable*)".

112 *on the answer . . . you* – "on the return thrust he hits you".

113 *Sophy* – "the Shah of Persia". See II.v.153.

114 *Pox on 't* was a curse. Similarly *Plague on 't* in line 246.

115 *fence* – "fencing".

174

FABIAN

Nothing of that wonderful promise, to read him by his form,[103] as you are like[104] to find him in the proof of his valour. 230
He is indeed, sir, the most skilful, bloody, and fatal opposite that
you could possibly have found in any part of Illyria. Will you
walk towards him? I will make your peace with him if I can.

VIOLA

I shall be much bound[105] to you for 't; I am one that had
rather go with sir priest than sir knight;[106] I care not who 235
knows so much of my mettle.

[*Exeunt*[107]

Re-enter SIR TOBY *with* SIR ANDREW

SIR TOBY

Why, man, he's a very devil; I have not seen such a firago.[108]
I had a pass[109] with him, rapier, scabbard, and all, and he gives
me the stuck-in[110] with such a mortal motion that it is inevitable;[111] and on the answer, he pays you[112] as surely as your 240
feet hit the ground they step on. They say he has been fencer
to the Sophy.[113]

SIR ANDREW

Pox on 't,[114] I 'll not meddle with him.

SIR TOBY

Ay, but he will not now be pacified; Fabian can scarce hold
him yonder. 245

SIR ANDREW

Plague on 't; an I thought he had been valiant and so cunning
in fence[115] I 'd have seen him damned ere I 'd have challenged
him. Let him let the matter slip, and I 'll give him my horse,
grey Capilet.

116 *motion* – "proposal".

117 *I'll ride . . . you* – "I'll take your horse (for riding) as well as I 'ride' (make a fool of) you".

118 *to take up the quarrel* – "with which to settle the quarrel".

119 *He is . . . him* – "He (Sir Andrew) is just as frightened of him (the youth)".

120 *for's* – "for his".

121 *he hath . . . his quarrel* – "he has thought again about the reason for his quarrel with you".

122 *supportance* – "upholding".

123 *Give ground* – "Move backwards".

124 *by the duello* – "by the laws of duelling".

SIR TOBY

I 'll make the motion.[116] Stand here; make a good show on 't; 250
this shall end without the perdition of souls. [*Aside*] Marry,
I 'll ride your horse as well as I ride you.[117]

Re-enter FABIAN *and* VIOLA

[*To* FABIAN] I have his horse to take up the quarrel.[118] I have
persuaded him the youth 's a devil.

FABIAN

[*To* SIR TOBY] He is as horribly conceited of him;[119] and pants 255
and looks pale, as if a bear were at his heels.

SIR TOBY

[*To* VIOLA] There 's no remedy, sir; he will fight with you
for 's[120] oath sake. Marry, he hath better bethought him of his
quarrel,[121] and he finds that now scarce to be worth talking of;
therefore draw for the supportance[122] of his vow; he protests he 260
will not hurt you.

VIOLA

[*Aside*] Pray God defend me! A little thing would make me tell
them how much I lack of a man.

FABIAN

[*To* VIOLA] Give ground,[123] if you see him furious.

SIR TOBY

Come, Sir Andrew, there 's no remedy; the gentleman will, 265
for his honour's sake, have one bout with you; he cannot by the
duello[124] avoid it; but he has promised me, as he is a gentleman
and a soldier, he will not hurt you. Come on; to 't.

SIR ANDREW

Pray God, he keep his oath!   [*Draws his sword*

125 *undertaker* – "one who acts on behalf of another", e.g. by fighting
for one side in a challenge.
126 *officers*, i.e. Orsino's state officers,
responsible for keeping order.

127 *He*, i.e. Capilet, his horse, which
he promised to give in return for
peace between them (lines 248–9).

VIOLA

I do assure you, 't is against my will.   [*Draws his sword* 270

Enter ANTONIO

ANTONIO

Put up your sword. If this young gentleman
Have done offence, I take the fault on me;
If you offend him, I for him defy you.   [*Drawing his sword*

SIR TOBY

You, sir! Why, what are you?

ANTONIO

One, sir, that for his love dares yet do more   275
Than you have heard him brag to you he will.

SIR TOBY

Nay, if you be an undertaker,[125] I am for you.   [*Draws*

FABIAN

O good Sir Toby, hold! Here come the officers.[126]

SIR TOBY

I 'll be with you anon.

VIOLA

Pray, sir, put your sword up, if you please.   280

SIR ANDREW

Marry, will I, sir; and, for that I promised you, I 'll be as good
as my word. He[127] will bear you easily, and reins well.

179

128 *favour* – "appearance".
129 *You stand amazed* – "You stand there looking very surprised", because, of course, the purse was given not to her but to Sebastian, her twin brother.

130 *my lean and low ability* – "the small amount I am able to give".
131 *my having is* – "my possessions are".
132 *I'll make . . . you*–"I'll divide with you what I have at present".
133 *coffer* – "(money in my) purse".

Enter two Officers

FIRST OFFICER

This is the man; do thy office.

SECOND OFFICER

Antonio, I arrest thee at the suit
Of Count Orsino.

ANTONIO

You do mistake me, sir.   285

FIRST OFFICER

No, sir, no jot; I know your favour[128] well,
Though now you have no sea-cap on your head.
Take him away; he knows I know him well.

ANTONIO

I must obey. [*To* VIOLA] This comes with seeking you;
But there 's no remedy; I shall answer it.   290
What will you do, now my necessity
Makes me to ask you for my purse? It grieves me
Much more for what I cannot do for you
Than what befalls myself. You stand amazed;[129]
But be of comfort.   295

SECOND OFFICER

Come, sir, away.

ANTONIO

I must entreat of you some of that money.

VIOLA

What money, sir?
For the fair kindness you have showed me here,
And part, being prompted by your present trouble,   300
Out of my lean and low ability[130]
I 'll lend you something; my having is[131] not much;
I 'll make division of my present with you.[132]
Hold, here is half my coffer.[133]

181

134 *my deserts . . . persuasion* – "what I deserve of you is not sufficient to persuade you".

135 *Lest that* – "in case".

136 *unsound* – "bad", since it would look as if he had helped his friend in order to be rewarded.

137 *vainness* – "boasting".

138 *Most venerable worth* – "to be worthy of great respect".

139 *vile* – "worthless".

140 *done good feature shame* – "shamed a good appearance".

ANTONIO

                   Will you deny me now?
Is 't possible that my deserts to you   305
Can lack persuasion?[134] Do not tempt my misery,
Lest that[135] it make me so unsound[136] a man
As to upbraid you with those kindnesses
That I have done for you.

VIOLA

                 I know of none;
Nor know I you by voice or any feature.   310
I hate ingratitude more in a man
Than lying, vainness,[137] babbling drunkenness,
Or any taint of vice whose strong corruption
Inhabits our frail blood.

ANTONIO

          O heavens themselves!

SECOND OFFICER

Come, sir, I pray you, go.   315

ANTONIO

Let me speak a little. This youth that you see here
I snatched one-half out of the jaws of death,
Relieved him with such sanctity of love,
And to his image, which methought did promise
Most venerable worth,[138] did I devotion.   320

FIRST OFFICER

What 's that to us? The time goes by; away!

ANTONIO

But O! how vile[139] an idol proves this god!
Thou hast, Sebastian, done good feature shame[140]

141 *unkind* – "unnatural, hard-hearted".

142 *the beauteous . . . devil* – "those who are beautiful to look at but bad inside are empty chests richly decorated by the devil".

143 *do from . . . fly* – "spring from such real feeling".

144 *so do not I* – "*I* do not believe (what I hear and what it leads me to imagine)".

145 *we'll whisper . . . saws*, perhaps to make fun of Antonio's moralising before he is led away.

146 *living in my glass*; when she looks in the glass she seems to see her brother, who is exactly like her.

147 *if it prove* – "if it should prove to be so".

148 *for* – "as for".

In nature there 's no blemish but the mind;
None can be called deformed but the unkind;[141]   325
Virtue is beauty, but the beauteous evil
Are empty trunks o'erflourished by the devil.[142]

FIRST OFFICER

The man grows mad; away with him! Come, come, sir.

ANTONIO

Lead me on.

[*Exeunt* Officers *with* ANTONIO

VIOLA

Methinks his words do from such passion fly,[143]   330
That he believes himself; so do not I.[144]
Prove true, imagination, O! prove true,
That I, dear brother, be now ta'en for you.

SIR TOBY

Come hither, knight; come hither, Fabian; we 'll whisper o'er
a couplet or two of most sage saws.[145]   335

VIOLA

He named Sebastian; I my brother know
Yet living in my glass;[146] even such and so
In favour was my brother; and he went
Still in this fashion, colour, ornament,
For him I imitate. O! if it prove,[147]   340
Tempests are kind, and salt waves fresh in love.

[*Exit*

SIR TOBY

A very dishonest paltry boy, and more a coward than a hare.
His dishonesty appears in leaving his friend here in necessity,
and denying him; and for[148] his cowardship, ask Fabian.

185

149 *religious in it* – "devoted to it".
150 *'Slid* was a swear-word; like *'Slight* at II.v.27, it is a shortened form of *God's light*.

151 *I'll after* – "I'll follow".
152 *event* – "result".
153 *I dare . . . yet* – "I bet any money that it (the result) will be nothing at all".

FABIAN

A coward, a most devout coward, religious in it.[149]   345

SIR ANDREW

'Slid,[150] I 'll after[151] him again, and beat him.

SIR TOBY

Do; cuff him soundly, but never draw thy sword.

SIR ANDREW

An I do not, –

[*Exit*

FABIAN

Come, let 's see the event.[152]

SIR TOBY

I dare lay any money 't will be nothing yet.[153]

[*Exeunt*   350

(IV.i) Feste, thinking that Sebastian is "Cesario", tells him Olivia wants to see him. Sebastian cannot guess why, and is further surprised when Sir Andrew, taking him to be "Cesario", comes up and hits him. He defends himself, and when Toby comes, they both draw their swords ready for a fight. Olivia enters and orders them to stop; she then takes Sebastian with her into the house.

1 *Will you* – "Do you want to".
2 *Go to* – "Come, come!", said in disapproval.
3 *held out* – "pretended".
4 *vent* – "speak out".
5 *of* – "from", *vent* seeming to him an affected expression; he repeats it mockingly in line 13.

6 *I am afraid . . . cockney* – "I fear that this great foolish fellow (*lubber*), the world, will turn out to be an affected person (*cockney*)", since it looks as if everything is affecting to be what it is not.
7 *ungird thy strangeness* – "stop pretending you do not know me".
8 *Greek* – "merry fellow".

188

ACT FOUR

Scene I. The Street before Olivia's House.
Enter SEBASTIAN *and* FESTE.

FESTE

Will you[1] make me believe that I am not sent for you?

SEBASTIAN

Go to,[2] go to; thou are a foolish fellow;
Let me be clear of thee.

FESTE

Well held out,[3] i' faith! No, I do not know you; nor I am not
sent to you by my lady to bid you come speak with her; nor   5
your name is not Master Cesario; nor this is not my nose neither.
Nothing that is so is so.

SEBASTIAN

I prithee, vent[4] thy folly somewhere else;
Thou know'st not me.

FESTE

Vent my folly! He has heard that word of[5] some great man,   10
and now applies it to a fool. Vent my folly! I am afraid this
great lubber, the world, will prove a cockney.[6] I prithee now,
ungird thy strangeness[7] and tell me what I shall vent to my
lady. Shall I vent to her that thou art coming?

SEBASTIAN

I prithee, foolish Greek,[8] depart from me;   15
There 's money for thee; if you tarry longer
I shall give worse payment.

189

9 *open* – "generous". Feste thinks this is another gift from Viola; see III.i.37.

10 *a good report . . . purchase* – "a good reputation – after payment over a long period"; *fourteen years' purchase* must refer to the cost of land at the time.

11 *there.* Sebastian hits Sir Andrew each time he says *there* in this line.

12 *in some . . . twopence* – "in the position of some of you for any money".

13 *Come on* – "Come away".

190

FESTE

By my troth, thou hast an open[9] hand. These wise men that
give fools money get themselves a good report – after four-
teen years' purchase.[10]   20

Enter SIR ANDREW

SIR ANDREW

Now, sir, have I met you again? There 's for you.

> [*Striking* SEBASTIAN

SEBASTIAN

Why, there 's for thee, and there, and there.[11]

> [*Beating* SIR ANDREW

Are all the people mad?

Enter SIR TOBY *and* FABIAN

SIR TOBY

Hold, sir, or I 'll throw your dagger o'er the house.

> [*They seize* SEBASTIAN

FESTE

This will I tell my lady straight. I would not be in some of your   25
coats for twopence.[12]

SIR TOBY

Come on,[13] sir; hold.

SIR ANDREW

Nay, let him alone; I 'll go another way to work with him; I 'll
have an action of battery against him if there be any law in
Illyria. Though I struck him first, yet it 's no matter for that.   30

SEBASTIAN

Let go thy hand.

14 *iron* – "sword", which had fallen when Sebastian knocked Sir Andrew down.

15 *you are well fleshed* – "you have experienced some blood".

16 *malapert* – "saucy".

17 *Ungracious* – "Ill-mannered".

18 *preached* – "taught".

19 *Rudesby* – a derisive name for an ill-mannered person. It is constructed from *rude*.

20 *sway . . . peace* – "govern what you do in dealing with this uncivil and unjust attack (*extent*) upon your peace".

21 *hear thou* – "hear".

22 *fruitless* – "pointless".

23 *Thou shalt . . . go* – "You *must* come (with me)".

24 *Beshrew* – "Curse".

25 *started . . . thee* – "stirred half my own poor heart in you", with some play on *hart* as a creature of the hunt. See I.i.16–17.

192

SIR TOBY

Come, sir, I will not let you go. Come, my young soldier, put
up your iron;[14] you are well fleshed;[15] come on.

SEBASTIAN

I will be free from thee. What would'st thou now?
If thou dar'st tempt me further, draw thy sword.   35

SIR TOBY

What, what! Nay, then I must have an ounce or two of this
malapert[16] blood from you.   [*Draws his sword*

Enter OLIVIA

OLIVIA

Hold, Toby! On thy life I charge thee, hold!

SIR TOBY

Madam!

OLIVIA

Will it be ever thus? Ungracious[17] wretch!   40
Fit for the mountains and the barbarous caves,
Where manners ne'er were preached.[18] Out of my sight!
Be not offended, dear Cesario.
[*To* SIR TOBY] Rudesby,[19] be gone!
                    [*Exeunt* SIR TOBY, SIR ANDREW, *and* FABIAN
                                        I prithee, gentle friend,
Let thy fair wisdom, not thy passion, sway   45
In this uncivil and unjust extent
Against thy peace.[20] Go with me to my house,
And hear thou[21] there how many fruitless[22] pranks
This ruffian hath botched up, that thou thereby
May'st smile at this. Thou shalt not choose but go;[23]   50
Do not deny. Beshrew[24] his soul for me,
He started one poor heart of mine in thee.[25]

26 *What relish . . . stream* – "What does
all this mean? (*relish* here means
'taste'). Where is it all leading to?"

27 *Or* – "Either".

28 *Let fancy . . . steep* – "Let love (*fancy*)
continue to soak my senses in the
waters of Lethe". Lethe was thought
to be a river of the underworld
whose waters brought forgetful-
ness.

(IV.ii) Malvolio has been put into a dark room. Feste, acting the part of a
priest, pretends to reason with him, but in fact baits him mercilessly. Feste
then talks to Malvolio in his own voice and agrees to bring him light and
writing materials.

1 *gown . . . beard.* Feste is going to
dress up as a priest by putting on
the black gown and the false beard
which Maria gives him.

2 *Sir Topas the curate; curate* – "priest".
The topaz, a precious stone, was
thought to be useful in the treatment of madness, and Topas is
therefore a fitting name for the
priest who visits the supposedly
mad Malvolio.

3 *the whilst* – "in the meantime".

4 *dissemble* – "disguise".

5 *dissembled* is here used in its modern
sense, "deceive". People, he suggests, sometimes wear the gown of
a priest without acting as a priest
should.

6 *tall* – "fine and handsome".

7 *said* – "called".

8 *a good housekeeper* – "a person who
keeps a good house", i.e. lives well
and is hospitable.

9 *goes as fairly* – "is as fitting (for a
priest)".

10 *careful* – "sparing".

11 *competitors* – "partners".

194

SEBASTIAN

What relish is in this? How runs the stream?²⁶
Or²⁷ I am mad, or else this is a dream.
Let fancy still my sense in Lethe steep;²⁸   55
If it be thus to dream, still let me sleep!

OLIVIA

Nay; come, I prithee; would thou 'dst be ruled by me!

SEBASTIAN

Madam, I will.

OLIVIA

O! say so, and so be.

[*Exeunt*

Scene II. A Room in Olivia's House.
Enter MARIA *and* FESTE.

MARIA

Nay, I prithee, put on this gown and this beard,¹ make him
believe thou art Sir Topas the curate;² do it quickly; I 'll call
Sir Toby the whilst.³

[*Exit*

FESTE

Well, I 'll put it on, and I will dissemble⁴ myself in 't; and I
would I were the first that ever dissembled⁵ in such a gown. I   5
am not tall⁶ enough to become the function well, nor lean
enough to be thought a good student; but to be said⁷ an honest
man and a good housekeeper⁸ goes as fairly⁹ as to say a careful¹⁰
man and a great scholar. The competitors¹¹ enter.

12 *Bonos dies* (Latin or Spanish) – "Good day".

13 *the old hermit of Prague . . . a niece of King Gorboduc.* These people are Feste's inventions; they have high-sounding names, but do not appear to be historical. (King Gorboduc was, however, an early British king.) See I.v.30 and II.iii.20–1 for more of Feste's names.

14 *Peace*, i.e. "May there be God's peace".

15 *hyperbolical* – (perhaps) "excessive in power".

Enter SIR TOBY BELCH *and* MARIA

SIR TOBY

Jove bless thee, Master Parson.   10

FESTE

Bonos dies,[12] Sir Toby; for, as the old hermit of Prague, that
never saw pen and ink, very wittily said to a niece of King
Gorboduc,[13] "That that is is"; so I, being Master Parson, am
Master Parson, for what is "that" but "that", and "is" but "is"?

SIR TOBY

To him, Sir Topas.   15

FESTE

[*Calling*] What ho! I say. Peace[14] in this prison.

SIR TOBY

The knave counterfeits well; a good knave.

MALVOLIO

[*Calling from within*] Who calls there?

FESTE

Sir Topas the curate, who comes to visit Malvolio the lunatic.

MALVOLIO

Sir Topas, Sir Topas, good Sir Topas, go to my lady.   20

FESTE

Out, hyperbolical[15] fiend! How vexest thou this man! Talkest
thou nothing but of ladies?

SIR TOBY

Well said, Master Parson.

197

16 *laid* – "made me live".

17 *modest* – "moderate".

18 *will use* – "wish to treat".

19 *house* – "place", i.e. the prison and the rooms near it.

20 *barricadoes* – "barricades", which would, of course, shut out the light.

21 *south-north* is meaningless; it is formed jokingly on such words as *south-east, north-west*.

22 *obstruction* – (*a*) "blocking out (of light)", and (*b*) "imprisonment, prevention of movement".

23 *more puzzled . . . fog* – "more confused than the Egyptians were in the fog"; a story in the Bible tells how a fog, "darkness which may be felt", came over Egypt for three days.

24 *abused* – "badly treated".

25 *make the trial . . . question* – "test this by debating (some point) with me".

26 *Pythagoras*, an ancient Greek philosopher, is said to have believed that on the death of a body the soul entered a new body, either human or animal and of the same or a different kind.

198

MALVOLIO

Sir Topas, never was man thus wronged. Good Sir Topas, do
not think I am mad; they have laid[16] me here in hideous dark-   25
ness.

FESTE

Fie, thou dishonest Satan! I call thee by the most modest[17]
terms; for I am one of those gentle ones that will use[18] the devil
himself with courtesy. Sayest thou that house[19] is dark?

MALVOLIO

As hell, Sir Topas.   30

FESTE

Why, it hath bay windows transparent as barricadoes,[20] and
the clerestories toward the south-north[21] are as lustrous as
ebony; and yet complainest thou of obstruction?[22]

MALVOLIO

I am not mad, Sir Topas. I say to you, this house is dark.

FESTE

Madman, thou errest; I say there is no darkness but ignorance,   35
in which thou art more puzzled than the Egyptians in their
fog.[23]

MALVOLIO

I say this house is as dark as ignorance, though ignorance were
as dark as hell; and I say there was never man thus abused.[24] I
am no more mad than you are; make the trial of it in any con-   40
stant question.[25]

FESTE

What is the opinion of Pythagoras[26] concerning wild fowl?

27 *grandam* – "grandmother".
28 *allow of thy wits* – "agree that you are not mad".
29 *I am . . . waters* – "I am ready for anything".
30 *To him* – "Go to him".
31 *knavery* – "stupid joking".
32 *If he . . . delivered* – "If he can be set free (*delivered*) easily".

33 *I cannot . . . upshot* – "I cannot take part in this game to its conclusion (*upshot*)". It is likely that Sir Toby and Maria are by this time secretly married; this would explain why Sir Toby is "now so far in offence" with Olivia.

MALVOLIO

That the soul of our grandam[27] might haply inhabit a bird.

FESTE

What thinkest thou of his opinion?

MALVOLIO

I think nobly of the soul, and no way approve his opinion.   45

FESTE

Fare thee well; remain thou still in darkness. Thou shalt hold
the opinion of Pythagoras ere I will allow of thy wits,[28] and
fear to kill a woodcock, lest thou dispossess the soul of thy grandam. Fare thee well.

MALVOLIO

Sir Topas! Sir Topas!   50

SIR TOBY

My most exquisite Sir Topas!

FESTE

[*To* SIR TOBY] Nay, I am for all waters.[29]

MARIA

Thou might'st have done this without thy beard and gown;
he sees thee not.

SIR TOBY

To him[30] in thine own voice, and bring me word how thou   55
findest him. [*To* MARIA] I would we were well rid of this
knavery.[31] If he may be conveniently delivered,[32] I would he
were; for I am now so far in offence with my niece that I cannot pursue with any safety this sport to the upshot.[33] Come by
and by to my chamber.   60

[*Exeunt* SIR TOBY *and* MARIA

201

34 *Hey Robin* . . . is the beginning of a song popular in Shakespeare's day.

35 *how thy lady does* – "how your lady is".

36 *perdy* – "indeed" (originally a French expression meaning "by God").

37 *as ever* . . . *hand* – "if you ever want to deserve well of me", i.e. to do something which will really call for a reward.

38 *help me to* – "get me".

39 *how fell you* . . . *wits?* – "how do you come to be out of your wits?" There were thought to be five distinct "wits" or powers of the mind.

FESTE

[*Singing*]   *Hey Robin, jolly Robin,*[34]
        Tell me how thy lady does.[35]

MALVOLIO

Fool!

FESTE

My lady is unkind, perdy.[36]

MALVOLIO

Fool!   65

FESTE

Alas! why is she so?

MALVOLIO

Fool, I say!

FESTE

She loves another.
        Who calls, ha?

MALVOLIO

Good fool, as ever thou wilt deserve well at my hand,[37] help me 70
to[38] a candle, and pen, ink, and paper. As I am a gentleman, I
will live to be thankful to thee for 't.

FESTE

Master Malvolio!

MALVOLIO

Ay, good fool.

FESTE

Alas, sir, how fell you besides your five wits?[39]   75

40 *notoriously* – "shamefully".

41 *in my wits* – "sane", not "beside" his wits.

42 *But as well?* – "Only as well (and no more)?"

43 *propertied me* – "put me away", as if he were "properties", theatrical scenery.

44 *to face . . . wits* – "tell me to my face that I am out of my wits".

45 *Advise you* – "Take care of".

46 *endeavour thyself* – "try".

47 *bibble-babble* – "foolish talk".

48 *shent* – "scolded" (by Sir Topas).

204

MALVOLIO

Fool, there was never man so notoriously[40] abused; I am as well
in my wits,[41] fool, as thou art.

FESTE

But as well?[42] Then you are mad indeed, if you be no better in
your wits than a fool.

MALVOLIO

They have here propertied me;[43] keep me in darkness, send   80
ministers to me, asses! and do all they can to face me out of my
wits.[44]

FESTE

Advise you[45] what you say; the minister is here. [*As* SIR TOPAS]
Malvolio, Malvolio, thy wits the heavens restore! Endeavour
thyself[46] to sleep, and leave thy vain bibble-babble.[47]   85

MALVOLIO

Sir Topas!

FESTE

Maintain no words with him, good fellow. [*As* FESTE] Who, I,
sir? Not I, sir. God be wi' you, good Sir Topas. [*As* SIR TOPAS]
Marry, amen . . . [*As* FESTE] I will, sir, I will.

MALVOLIO

Fool, fool, fool, I say!   90

FESTE

Alas, sir, be patient. What say you, sir? I am shent[48] for speaking
to you.

MALVOLIO

Good fool, help me to some light and some paper; I tell thee I
am as well in my wits as any man in Illyria.

49 *Well-a-day* – "Alas".
50 *set down* – "write".
51 *advantage* – "profit".
52 *be gone* reminds Feste of an old song, *I am gone, sir*, which he sings as he makes his way out.
53 *the old Vice*. In the ancient religious plays of England a character called the Vice appeared with the devil; they fought with a thin wooden sword, and sometimes the Vice attempted to cut the devil's nails with it (see line 115). Feste compares himself to the Vice, and Malvolio, by suggestion, to the devil.

54 *Your need to sustain* – "to do as you wish", and perhaps, "to treat you as the Vice treats the devil".
55 *goodman devil* – "master devil", a merry and polite way of saying farewell to Malvolio.

Like to the old Vice[53]

206

FESTE

Well-a-day,[49] that you were, sir!   95

MALVOLIO

By this hand, I am. Good fool, some ink, paper, and light;
and convey what I will set down[50] to my lady; it shall advantage[51] thee more than ever the bearing of letter did.

FESTE

I will help you to 't. But tell me true, are you not mad indeed,
or do you but counterfeit?   100

MALVOLIO

Believe me, I am not; I tell thee true.

FESTE

Nay, I 'll ne'er believe a madman till I see his brains. I will
fetch you light and paper and ink.

MALVOLIO

Fool, I 'll requite it in the highest degree; I prithee, be gone.[52]

FESTE

[Singing]   *I am gone, sir,*   105
                              And anon, sir,
                        I 'll be with you again,
                              In a trice
                           Like to the old Vice,[53]
                        Your need to sustain;[54]   110

                        Who with dagger of lath,
                        In his rage and his wrath,
                           Cries, Ah, ha! to the devil;
                        Like a mad lad,
                        Pare thy nails, dad;   115
                           Adieu, goodman devil.[55]   [*Exit*

(iv.iii) Olivia brings in a priest, and, to Sebastian's great surprise, arranges that they shall be married at once.

1 *she*, i.e. Olivia, who has mistaken Sebastian for "Cesario".
2 *was* – "had been".
3 *found this credit* – "found it generally believed".
4 *this accident . . . fortune* – "this accident of abundant good fortune".
5 *instance* – "previous example".
6 *discourse* – "reason".
7 *wrangle* – "argue".
8 *trust* – "belief".

9 *sway* – "rule".
10 *Take . . . dispatch* – "Attend to (household) business and see that it is carried out".
11 *stable bearing* – "self-assured manner".
12 *deceivable* – "deceptive".
13 *the chantry by* – "the chapel close by".
14 *doubtful* – "suspicious".

Scene III. Olivia's Garden.
Enter SEBASTIAN.

SEBASTIAN

This is the air; that is the glorious sun;
This pearl she[1] gave me, I do feel 't and see 't;
And though 't is wonder that enwraps me thus,
Yet 't is not madness. Where 's Antonio then?
I could not find him at the Elephant;   5
Yet there he was,[2] and there I found this credit,[3]
That he did range the town to seek me out.
His counsel now might do me golden service;
For though my soul disputes well with my sense
That this may be some error, but no madness,   10
Yet doth this accident and flood of fortune[4]
So far exceed all instance,[5] all discourse,[6]
That I am ready to distrust mine eyes,
And wrangle[7] with my reason that persuades me
To any other trust[8] but that I am mad   15
Or else the lady 's mad; yet if 't were so,
She could not sway[9] her house, command her followers,
Take and give back affairs and their dispatch[10]
With such a smooth, discreet, and stable bearing[11]
As I perceive she does. There 's something in 't   20
That is deceivable.[12] But here the lady comes.

Enter OLIVIA *and a* Priest

OLIVIA

Blame not this haste of mine. If you mean well,
Now go with me and with this holy man
Into the chantry by;[13] there, before him,
And underneath that consecrated roof,   25
Plight me the full assurance of your faith,
That my most jealous and too doubtful[14] soul
May live at peace. He shall conceal it

209

15 *conceal it Whiles* – "keep it a secret until".

16 *come to note* – "become generally known".

17 *What time* – "and then".

18 *celebration* – "marriage ceremony".

19 *birth* – "my social position".

20 *fairly note* – "look favourably upon".

Whiles[15] you are willing it shall come to note,[16]
What time [17] we will our celebration[18] keep   30
According to my birth.[19] What do you say?

SEBASTIAN

I 'll follow this good man, and go with you;
And, having sworn truth, ever will be true.

OLIVIA

Then lead the way, good father; and heavens so shine
That they may fairly note[20] this act of mine!   35

[*Exeunt*

(v.i) Duke Orsino and his attendants arrive at Olivia's house. Antonio is brought in a prisoner, and the Duke recognizes him as an enemy of the state; but Viola, whom Antonio helped at the time of the duel with Sir Andrew, pleads for him. When Olivia comes, Viola must choose between her and the Duke. She declares her love for the Duke, and to Olivia this is inexplicable because she believes she is already married to "Cesario"; she even brings back the priest to prove it. Sir Toby and Sir Andrew, meanwhile, have suffered badly from fights with Sebastian, whom they took for "Cesario". When Sebastian arrives, he tries to tell Olivia why he has hurt Toby and Andrew; but everyone looks at him and Viola, and sees that they are exactly alike. Then all the mistakes are explained. Feste brings in the letter which Malvolio has written from prison; it shows that he is not really mad, and this leads Fabian to admit that he and the others were responsible for tricking Malvolio. The Duke finishes the action of the play by asking Viola to marry him.

1 *to give . . . again*. This refers to a true story told of Queen Elizabeth I. A relative of hers, Dr Bullein, had a dog which he loved dearly. The queen, knowing of this, told him she would ask something of him, and promised to give him anything he asked in return. She asked him for his dog and he gave it to her. Then, reminding her of her promise, he asked her to give it back again to him.

ACT FIVE

Scene I. *The Street before Olivia's House.*
Enter FESTE *and* FABIAN.

FABIAN

Now, as thou lovest me, let me see his letter.

FESTE

Good Master Fabian, grant me another request.

FABIAN

Any thing.

FESTE

Do not desire to see this letter.

FABIAN

This is, to give a dog, and in recompense desire my dog again.[1] 5

Enter DUKE, VIOLA, CURIO, *and* Attendants

DUKE

Belong you to the Lady Olivia, friends?

FESTE

Ay, sir; we are some of her trappings.

DUKE

I know thee well; how dost thou, my good fellow?

FESTE

Truly, sir, the better for my foes and the worse for my friends.

DUKE

Just the contrary; the better for thy friends. 10

213

2 *and make* – "and by doing so make".

3 *profit in* – "gain in".

4 *abused* – "deceived".

5 *conclusions to be* (line 16) . . . *foes* – "comparing conclusions with kisses, if you take four negatives to make two affirmatives, then I am the worse for my friends and the better for my enemies". He seems to mean that, as kisses are double things (made with two lips or two mouths), so he is stating his conclusions in doubles: it was once thought to be a grammatical rule that two negatives make one affirmative. The two negatives – he is not, as one might expect, worse for his enemies, nor is he better for his friends – suggest the affirmative that he is called, and is in fact, an ass.

6 *my friends*, and therefore likely to flatter instead of speaking the truth.

7 *double-dealing* – "giving twice over", and also "deceit".

8 *ill counsel* – "bad advice", taking *double-dealing* in the sense "deceit".

9 *your grace* – "your good nature", and follow, for once, *ill counsel*, as in the line before. But Feste also plays on the title "Your Grace", used in addressing a duke.

10 *flesh and blood* – "body and soul".

FESTE

No, sir, the worse.

DUKE

How can that be?

FESTE

Marry, sir, they praise me and make[2] an ass of me; now my foes
tell me plainly I am an ass; so that by my foes, sir, I profit in[3]
the knowledge of myself, and by my friends I am abused;[4] so   15
that, conclusions to be as kisses, if your four negatives make
your two affirmatives, why then, the worse for my friends and
and better for my foes.[5]

DUKE

Why, this is excellent.

FESTE

By my troth, sir, no; though it please you to be one of my   20
friends.[6]

DUKE

Thou shalt not be the worse for me; there's gold.
                                                    [Gives him money

FESTE

But that it would be double-dealing,[7] sir, I would you could
make it another.

DUKE

O! you give me ill counsel.[8]   25

FESTE

Put your grace[9] in your pocket, sir, for this once, and let your
flesh and blood[10] obey it.

11 *to be* – "as to be".

12 *Primo, secundo, tertio* – "First, second, third", words once used in a dice game. Feste is now asking for a third piece of gold.

13 *play* – "game".

14 *the third pays for all* – "the third time is lucky", a proverb used to encourage people who have failed twice in something to try once more.

15 *triplex* – a rhythm of three beats in music.

16 *tripping measure* – "rhythm for dancing".

17 *the bells of Saint Bennet*. A church of St. Bennet or Benedict stood near Shakespeare's theatre, the Globe, in London, and perhaps it had three bells.

18 *put you in mind* – "remind you".

19 *at this throw* – "on this occasion", but also with a joke on the throwing of a dice (continuing Feste's *Primo, secundo . . .* in line 30).

20 *lullaby to you bounty* – "May your bounty sleep well" suggested by *awake* in the line before.

21 *Vulcan*, the Roman god of fire, often represented as a blacksmith.

22 *baubling* – "unimportant".

23 *unprizable* – "too small to measure".

24 *scathful grapple* – "destructive warfare".

25 *bottom* – "ship".

26 *very envy . . . him* – "even those who envied him his courage and those who suffered loss declared his fame and honour". His ship was very small, yet he fought bravely against them.

With which such scathful grapple[24] *did he make*
With the most noble bottom[25] *of our fleet*

216

DUKE

[*Giving him more money*] Well, I will be so much a sinner to be[11]
a double-dealer; there 's another.

FESTE

Primo, secundo, tertio,[12] is a good play;[13] and the old saying is, the   30
third pays for all;[14] the *triplex*,[15] sir, is a good tripping measure;[16] or the bells of Saint Bennet,[17] sir, may put you in mind:[18]
one, two, three.

DUKE

You can fool no more money out of me at this throw;[19] if you
will let your lady know I am here to speak with her, and bring   35
her along with you, it may awake my bounty further.

FESTE

Marry, sir, lullaby to your bounty[20] till I come again. I go, sir;
but I would not have you to think that my desire of having is
the sin of covetousness; but as you say, sir, let your bounty
take a nap; I will awake it anon.   40

[*Exit*

VIOLA

Here comes the man, sir, that did rescue me.

Enter ANTONIO *and* Officers

DUKE

That face of his I do remember well;
Yet, when I saw it last, it was besmeared
As black as Vulcan[21] in the smoke of war.
A baubling[22] vessel was he captain of,   45
For shallow draught and bulk unprizable;[23]
With which such scathful grapple[24] did he make
With the most noble bottom[25] of our fleet,
That very envy and the tongue of loss
Cried fame and honour on him.[26] What 's the matter?   50

217

27 *took* – "captured".
28 *Phoenix*, the name of a ship; so also *Tiger* in line 53.
29 *fraught* – "goods carried in a ship".
30 *Candy* – "Crete".
31 *desperate . . . state* – "without regard for his character or the situation he is in".
32 *brabble* – "brawl".
33 *drew*, i.e. drew his sword
34 *put strange . . . me* – "spoke strangely to me".
35 *I know . . . distraction* – "I do not know what this (the cause of the *strange speech*) was, unless it was madness".
36 *Notable* – "Famous".

37 *in terms . . . dear* – "for causes so bloody and grievous".
38 *Be pleased that I* – "Allow me to".
39 *on base . . . enough* – "for sufficient, firm reason".
40 *rude* – "rough".
41 *redeem* – "save".
42 *his in dedication* – "given him for his own use".
43 *pure* – "entirely".
44 *Into* for *unto*, following *expose* in the line before.
45 *adverse* – "unfriendly".
46 *Where being apprehended* – "and when I was taken (prisoner) in this place".
47 *Not meaning to partake* – "since he did not intend to share".

FIRST OFFICER

Orsino, this is that Antonio
That took[27] the Phoenix[28] and her fraught[29] from Candy;[30]
And this is he that did the Tiger board,
When your young nephew Titus lost his leg.
Here in the streets, desperate of shame and state,[31]   55
In private brabble[32] did we apprehend him.

VIOLA

He did me kindness, sir, drew[33] on my side;
But in conclusion put strange speech upon me;[34]
I know not what 't was but distraction.[35]

DUKE

Notable[36] pirate! thou salt-water thief!   60
What foolish boldness brought thee to their mercies,
Whom thou, in terms so bloody and so dear,[37]
Hast made thine enemies?

ANTONIO

                             Orsino, noble sir,
Be pleased that I[38] shake off these names you give me;
Antonio never yet was thief or pirate,   65
Though I confess, on base and ground enough,[39]
Orsino's enemy. A witchcraft drew me hither;
That most ungrateful boy there by your side,
From the rude[40] sea's enraged and foamy mouth
Did I redeem;[41] a wreck past hope he was;   70
His life I gave him, and did thereto add
My love, without retention or restraint,
All his in dedication;[42] for his sake
Did I expose myself, pure[43] for his love,
Into[44] the danger of this adverse[45] town;   75
Drew to defend him when he was beset;
Where being apprehended,[46] his false cunning,
Not meaning to partake[47] with me in danger,

48 *to face . . . acquaintance* – "to look me in the face and yet pretend not to know me".

49 *grew . . . wink* – "became in a moment like someone who had not seen me for twenty years".

50 *recommended . . . use* – "persuaded him to use".

51 *vacancy* – "space".

52 *but that* – "except for that which".

Taught him to face me out of his acquaintance,[48]
And grew a twenty-years-removed thing   80
While one would wink,[49] denied me mine own purse,
Which I had recommended to his use[50]
Not half an hour before.

VIOLA

How can this be?

DUKE

When came he to this town?

ANTONIO

Today, my lord; and for three months before,   85
No interim, not a minute's vacancy,[51]
Both day and night did we keep company.

Enter OLIVIA *and* Attendants

DUKE

Here comes the countess; now heaven walks on earth!
[*To* ANTONIO] But for thee, fellow; fellow, thy words are
      madness;
Three months this youth hath tended upon me;   90
But more of that anon. [*To the* Officers] Take him aside.

OLIVIA

What would my lord, but that[52] he may not have,
Wherein Olivia may seem serviceable?
Cesario, you do not keep promise with me.

VIOLA

Madam!   95

DUKE

Gracious Olivia, –

221

53 *If it be . . . fulsome . . .* – "If it has anything (*aught*) to do with the old theme (of love), my lord, it is as coarse and wearisome . . ."

54 *ingrate* – "ungrateful".

55 *altars*. The idea of Orsino offering his love as a worshipper making an offering to a god is continued with *offerings* and *devotion* in the following lines.

56 *the Egyptian thief*. In a classical story, Thyamis, the leader of a band of robbers in Egypt, captures the beautiful Chariclea and, intending to marry her, shuts her up in a cave. He is attacked by another robber band, and, hoping to have Chariclea's company in the next world, rushes to kill her before he is himself killed. In the darkness of the cave, however, he kills another woman by mistake.

57 *savours nobly* – "has some nobility in it".

58 *Since you* (line 112) . . . *still* – "since you scornfully (*to non-regardance*) throw away my devotion, and since I know in part what it is (*the instrument*) that forces me from my proper place in your favour, live on as the cold and stony-hearted tyrant you are".

OLIVIA

What do you say, Cesario? Good my lord, –
[*Signs to prevent* ORSINO *from speaking*

VIOLA

My lord would speak; my duty hushes me.

OLIVIA

If it be aught to the old tune, my lord,
It is as fat and fulsome[53] to mine ear,   100
As howling after music.

DUKE

Still so cruel?

OLIVIA

Still so constant, lord.

DUKE

What, to perverseness? You uncivil lady,
To whose ingrate[54] and unauspicious altars[55]
My soul the faithfull'st offerings hath breathed out   105
That e'er devotion tendered! What shall I do?

OLIVIA

Even what it please my lord, that shall become him.

DUKE

Why should I not, had I the heart to do it,
Like to the Egyptian thief[56] at point of death,
Kill what I love? A savage jealousy   110
That sometimes savours nobly.[57] But hear me this:
Since you to non-regardance cast my faith,
And that I partly know the instrument
That screws me from my true place in your favour,
Live you the marble-breasted tyrant still;[58]   115

223

59 *I tender dearly* – "I regard most tenderly".
60 *in his master's spite* – "to annoy his master".
61 *jocund, apt* – "gaily, readily".
62 *do you rest* – "give you peace".

63 *you witnesses above*, i.e. the gods.
64 *Ay me, detested!* "Alas, (I am) witnessed against, abused with an oath"; Viola has sworn to the *witnesses above* the truth of what she said.

But this your minion, whom I know you love,
And whom, by heaven I swear, I tender dearly,[59]
Him will I tear out of that cruel eye,
Where he sits crownéd in his master's spite.[60]
[*To* VIOLA] Come, boy, with me; my thoughts are ripe in mis-
    chief;   120
I 'll sacrifice the lamb that I do love,
To spite a raven's heart within a dove.

VIOLA

And I, most jocund, apt,[61] and willingly,
To do you rest,[62] a thousand deaths would die.

OLIVIA

Where goes Cesario?

VIOLA

                     After him I love   125
More than I love these eyes, more than my life,
More, by all mores, than e'er I shall love wife.
If I do feign, you witnesses above,[63]
Punish my life for tainting of my love!

OLIVIA

Ah me, detested![64] how am I beguiled!   130

VIOLA

Who does beguile you? Who does do you wrong?

OLIVIA

Hast thou forgot thyself? Is it so long?
Call forth the holy father.

DUKE

[*To* VIOLA]   Come away!

65 *husband*. Olivia calls "Cesario" husband even before the full marriage ceremony, since the engagement, enacted before a priest, was taken to be most solemn and binding. This, not the marriage, is the plighted *assurance* at IV.iii.26 and the *contract* at line 147 of this scene.

66 *strangle thy propriety* – "kill your individuality", as a husband.

67 *that thou fear'st* – "him you fear" (i.e. Orsino), and also, possibly, "what you fear to become" (i.e. Olivia's husband).

68 *charge* – "bid".

69 *lately* – "recently".

70 *occasion now Reveals* – "circumstances now reveal".

71 *newly* – "just now".

72 *close of lips* – "kiss".

73 *interchangement . . . rings* – "exchange of rings" at the time of engagement.

226

OLIVIA

Whither, my lord? Cesario, husband,[65] stay.

DUKE

Husband!

OLIVIA

Ay, husband; can he that deny?   135

DUKE

Her husband, sirrah!

VIOLA

No, my lord, not I.

OLIVIA

Alas! it is the baseness of thy fear
That makes thee strangle thy propriety.[66]
Fear not, Cesario; take thy fortunes up;
Be that thou know'st thou art, and then thou art   140
As great as that thou fear'st.[67]

Enter PRIEST

                    O welcome, father!
Father, I charge[68] thee, by thy reverence,
Here to unfold, though lately[69] we intended
To keep in darkness what occasion now
Reveals[70] before 't is ripe, what thou dost know   145
Hath newly[71] passed between this youth and me.

PRIEST

A contract of eternal bond of love,
Confirmed by mutual joinder of your hands,
Attested by the holy close of lips,[72]
Strengthened by interchangement of your rings;[73]   150

227

74 *Sealed . . . testimony* – "sealed (i.e. declared as true) by me in my office as priest (*my function*) and by myself as witness (*my testimony*)".

75 *When time . . . case* – "when time has begun to turn your hair grey"; *grizzle* – "sprinkling of grey hairs"; *case* – "the skin or fur of an animal". (Orsino has just called Viola a cub.)

76 *Or will not . . . overthrow* – "Or otherwise (*else*) will your cunning not develop so quickly that you yourself will fall at the trip you planned for others?"; *trip* seems to be taken from the terms of wrestling.

77 *Hold little faith* – "Keep a little of your honour".

78 *a bloody coxcomb* – "a head covered with blood"; *coxcomb* is literally the crest of a cock.

And all the ceremony of this compact
Sealed in my function, by my testimony;[74]
Since when, my watch hath told me, toward my grave
I have travelled but two hours.

DUKE

O thou dissembling cub! what wilt thou be   155
When time hath sowed a grizzle on thy case?[75]
Or will not else thy craft so quickly grow
That thine own trip shall be thine overthrow?[76]
Farewell, and take her; but direct thy feet
Where thou and I henceforth may never meet.   160

VIOLA

My lord, I do protest, –

OLIVIA

O! do not swear;
Hold little faith,[77] though thou hast too much fear.

Enter SIR ANDREW AGUECHEEK

SIR ANDREW

For the love of God, a surgeon! Send one presently to Sir Toby.

OLIVIA

What 's the matter?

SIR ANDREW

He has broke my head across, and has given Sir Toby a bloody 165
coxcomb[78] too. For the love of God, your help! I had rather
than forty pound I were at home.

OLIVIA

Who has done this, Sir Andrew?

79 *incarnadine* is probably used ignorantly by Sir Andrew for *incarnate* – "in the flesh".

80 *'Od's lifelings!*, an expression used in swearing; literally it means "God's little life".

81 *that that ... Toby* – "what I did I was urged to do by Sir Toby".

82 *upon* – "against".

83 *bespake you fair* – "spoke fair words to you".

84 *set nothing by* – "think nothing of".

85 *halting* – "walking lame".

86 *in drink* – "drunk".

87 *tickled you othergates* – "dealt with you in another way".

88 *agone* – "ago".

89 *set* – "closed", as the sun and moon set and leave darkness.

SIR ANDREW

The count's gentleman, one Cesario; we took him for a cow-
ard, but he 's the very devil incardinate.[79]   170

DUKE

My gentleman, Cesario?

SIR ANDREW

'Od's lifelings![80] here he is. [*To* VIOLA] You broke my head for
nothing! And that that I did, I was set on to do 't by Sir Toby.[81]

VIOLA

Why do you speak to me? I never hurt you;
You drew your sword upon[82] me without cause;   175
But I bespake you fair,[83] and hurt you not.

SIR ANDREW

If a bloody coxcomb be a hurt, you *have* hurt me;
I think you set nothing by[84] a bloody coxcomb.

Enter SIR TOBY BELCH *and* FESTE

Here comes Sir Toby halting;[85] you shall hear more; but if he
had not been in drink[86] he would have tickled you other-   180
gates[87] than he did.

DUKE

How now, gentlemen! how is 't with you?

SIR TOBY

That 's all one; has hurt me, and there 's the end on 't. [*To*
FESTE] Sot, didst see Dick surgeon, sot?

FESTE

O! he 's drunk, Sir Toby, an hour agone;[88] his eyes were set[89] at   185
eight i' the morning.

90 *a passy-measures pavin*. It is suggested that this phrase is prompted in Sir Toby's mind by *set at eight* in the line before. A slow dance called the pavane (*pavin*) moved in measures of eight bars (i.e. was *set at eight*); *passy-measures*, the English form of an Italian phrase meaning "one and a half steps", was the name given to a certain kind of pavane. Sir Toby, half-drunk, is reminded of this dance, and, since it is slow and stately, he dislikes it and calls the surgeon by its name.

91 *dressed*, i.e. have their wounds dressed.

92 *an ass-head* ... Sir Toby begins to call Sir Andrew by insulting names.

93 *gull* – "fool".

94 *But had ... safety* – "But, having regard to my own safety (*with wit and safety*), I could have done no less than I did, even if he had been my own brother".

95 *You throw ... me* – "You look at me strangely".

96 *it*, i.e. what he has done to Sir Toby.

97 *habit* – "dress".

98 *A natural perspective*. Several kinds of manufactured objects were called *perspectives* in Shakespeare's day. It is impossible to say for certain which is referred to here, but the one meant is most likely that in which a picture appeared in various ways depending upon the angle from which it was looked at. This effect was probably obtained by putting together two pictures which were almost exactly alike; in the same way some kinds of advertisement made today change their appearance as one walks past them. In the play, the Duke sees in Viola and Sebastian a *perspective*, not man-made, but in nature.

A natural perspective,[98] *that is, and is not*

SIR TOBY

Then he 's a rogue, and a passy-measures pavin.[90] I hate a
drunken rogue.

OLIVIA

Away with him! Who hath made this havoc with them?

SIR ANDREW

I 'll help you, Sir Toby, because we 'll be dressed[91] together.   190

SIR TOBY

Will you help? An ass-head,[92] and a coxcomb, and a knave, a
thin-faced knave, a gull![93]

OLIVIA

Get him to bed, and let his hurt be looked to.
       [*Exeunt* FESTE, FABIAN, SIR TOBY, *and* SIR ANDREW

Enter SEBASTIAN

SEBASTIAN

I am sorry, madam, I have hurt your kinsman;
But had it been the brother of my blood,   195
I must have done no less with wit and safety.[94]
You throw a strange regard upon me,[95] and by that
I do perceive it[96] hath offended you;
Pardon me, sweet one, even for the vows
We made each other but so late ago.   200

DUKE

One face, one voice, one habit,[97] and two persons;
A natural perspective,[98] that is, and is not!

SEBASTIAN

Antonio! O my dear Antonio!
How have the hours racked and tortured me
Since I have lost thee!   205

99 *Fear'st thou that* – "Are you afraid
(that I am not)?"
100 *that deity . . . every where* – "the
god-like quality in my nature of
being here and everywhere else
(at the same time)".
101 *blind*, probably in the sense that
the waves could not see what they
were doing in taking the life of a
beautiful girl.
102 *Of charity* – "Out of your charity,
(tell me)".
103 *So went he suited* – "he went
dressed like this".

104 *suit* – "dress".
105 *fright* for *frighten*.
106 *in that . . . participate* – "clothed
materially (*grossly clad*) in that
body (*dimension*) which I acquired
as part of me (*did participate*) from
the womb"; it is only part of him,
since his whole being is body and
soul together.
107 *as . . . even* – "since everything else
fits (in suggesting that you are
Viola)".

234

SCENE I]

ANTONIO

Sebastian are you?

SEBASTIAN

Fear'st thou that,⁹⁹ Antonio?

ANTONIO

How have you made division of yourself?
An apple cleft in two is not more twin
Than these two creatures. Which is Sebastian?

OLIVIA

Most wonderful!   210

SEBASTIAN

[*Noticing* VIOLA] Do I stand there? I never had a brother;
Not can there be that deity in my nature,
Of here and every where.¹⁰⁰ I had a sister,
Whom the blind¹⁰¹ waves and surges have devoured.
[*To* VIOLA] Of charity,¹⁰² what kin are you to me?   215
What countryman, what name, what parentage?

VIOLA

Of Messaline; Sebastian was my father;
Such a Sebastian was my brother too,
So went he suited¹⁰³ to his watery tomb.
If spirits can assume both form and suit¹⁰⁴   220
You come to fright¹⁰⁵ us.

SEBASTIAN

                    A spirit I am indeed;
But am in that dimension grossly clad
Which from the womb I did participate.¹⁰⁶
Were you a woman, as the rest goes even,¹⁰⁷
I should my tears let fall upon your cheek,   225
And say "Thrice welcome, drownéd Viola!"

235

108 *that record is lively* – "that memory is (still) alive".
109 *nothing . . . both* – "nothing hinders us from making each other happy".
110 *do cohere . . . That* – "sticks and fits exactly, (proving) that".
111 *Where* – "at whose house".
112 *maiden weeds* – "girl's clothes".
113 *between* – "concerned with".

114 *mistook* for *mistaken*.
115 *But nature . . . that* – "but nature, as she is inclined to do, turned that (your mistake) to good account (*drew in that*)". A bias was a weight inside a bowl which, when the bowl was played, made it move in a curve; if well judged, this could be advantageous to the player.

VIOLA

My father had a mole upon his brow.

SEBASTIAN

And so had mine.

VIOLA

And died that day when Viola from her birth
Had numbered thirteen years.   230

SEBASTIAN

O! that record is lively[108] in my soul.
He finishéd indeed his mortal act
That day that made my sister thirteen years.

VIOLA

If nothing lets to make us happy both,[109]
But this my masculine usurped attire,   235
Do not embrace me till each circumstance
Of place, time, fortune, do cohere and jump
That[110] I am Viola; which to confirm,
I 'll bring you to a captain in this town,
Where[111] lie my maiden weeds;[112] by whose gentle help   240
I was preserved to serve this noble count.
All the occurrence of my fortune since
Hath been between[113] this lady and this lord.

SEBASTIAN

[To OLIVIA] So comes it, lady, you have been mistook,[114]
But nature to her bias drew in that.[115]   245
You would have been contracted to a maid;
Nor are you therein, by my life, deceived.
You are betrothed both to a maid and man.

237

116 *amazed* – "alarmed".
117 *glass*, i.e. the *perspective* in line 202.
118 *like to* – "as much as".
119 *over-swear* – "swear over again".
120 *As doth . . . night* – "as the sun's path (*that orbéd continent*) keeps the fire (i.e. the sun) which distinguishes day from night". So truly will Viola keep in her heart what she has sworn.

121 *upon some action* – "because of some legal action".
122 *in durance . . . suit* – "under arrest at Malvolio's accusation".
123 *enlarge him* – "set him free".
124 *distract* for *distracted*.
125 *A most . . . his* – "A strong distraction of my own drove his distraction completely (*clearly*) out of my mind"; *extracting* – "taking everything out (of the mind)".

238

DUKE

Be not amazed;[116] right noble is his blood.
If this be so, as yet the glass[117] seems true,   250
I shall have share in this most happy wreck.
[*To* VIOLA] Boy, thou hast said to me a thousand times
Thou never should'st love woman like to me.[118]

VIOLA

And all those sayings will I over-swear,[119]
And all those swearings keep as true in soul   255
As doth that orbéd continent the fire
That severs day from night.[120]

DUKE

               Give me thy hand;
And let me see thee in thy woman's weeds.

VIOLA

The captain that did bring me first on shore
Hath my maid's garments; he upon some action[121]   260
Is now in durance at Malvolio's suit,[122]
A gentleman, and follower of my lady's.

OLIVIA

He shall enlarge him.[123] Fetch Malvolio hither.
And yet, alas, now I remember me,
They say, poor gentleman, he is much distract.[124]   265
A most extracting frenzy of mine own
From my remembrance clearly banished his.[125]

Re-enter FESTE, *with a letter, and* FABIAN

[*To* FESTE] How does he, sirrah?

239

126 *Belzebub* – "the devil".
127 *at the stave's end* – "at a distance".
128 *case* – "condition".
129 *Has here writ* – "He has written here".
130 *epistles* – "letters". Feste plays on the word *epistles* (as meaning also readings from the Bible in church) by contrasting it with *gospels*.

131 *it skills not much* – "it does not much matter".
132 *delivers* – "speaks the words of".
133 *art thou mad?* He has evidently read the words in the way a madman might read them.
134 *vox* (Latin) – "the right voice", that of a madman.
135 *madonna*; see note 19 to I.v.
136 *perpend* – "attend".

240

FESTE

Truly, madam, he holds Belzebub[126] at the stave's end[127] as well
as a man in his case[128] may do. Has here writ[129] a letter to you; 270
I should have given it you today morning; but as a madman's
epistles[130] are no gospels, so it skills not much[131] when they are
delivered.

OLIVIA

Open 't, and read it.

FESTE

Look then to be well edified when the fool delivers[132] the mad- 275
man.
[*Reads*] *By the Lord, madam,* –

OLIVIA

How now! art *thou* mad?[133]

FESTE

No, madam, I do but read madness; an your ladyship will have
it as it ought to be, you must allow *vox*.[134]   280

OLIVIA

Prithee, read i' thy right wits.

FESTE

So I do, madonna;[135] but to read his right wits is to read thus;
therefore perpend,[136] my princess, and give ear.

OLIVIA

[*To* FABIAN] Read it *you*, sirrah.

FABIAN

[*Reading*] *By the Lord, madam, you wrong me, and the world shall* 285
know it; though you have put me into darkness, and given your
drunken cousin rule over me, yet have I the benefit of my senses as well

241

137 *induced . . . on* – "persuaded me to adopt the appearance (*semblance*) I did".

138 *I leave . . . injury* – "I neglect my duty a little (by not addressing you more respectfully), but speak out because of the wrongs done to me".

139 *This savours . . . distraction* – "This does not much suggest madness".

140 *delivered* – "set free".

141 *these things . . . on* – "when you have given more thought to these things".

142 *sister*, since her husband, Sebastian, is the brother of Viola, who may be Orsino's wife.

143 *One day . . . on 't* – "the double marriage (*alliance*, making Olivia a sister to Orsino) shall be completed in one day".

144 *proper* – "own".

145 *apt* – "ready".

146 *quits you* – "frees you from service".

147 *mettle* – "character".

148 *beneath . . . breeding* – "unworthy of your gentle and sheltered up-bringing".

149 *mistress* – "wife".

as your ladyship. I have your own letter that induced me to the sem-
blance I put on; [137] *with the which I doubt not but to do myself much*
right, or you much shame. Think of me as you please. I leave my duty 290
a little unthought of, and speak out of my injury.[138]

THE MADLY-USED MALVOLIO

OLIVIA

Did he write this?

FESTE

Ay, madam.

DUKE

This savours not much of distraction.[139]

OLIVIA

See him delivered,[140] Fabian; bring him hither.   295

[*Exit* FABIAN

My lord, so please you, these things further thought on,[141]
To think me as well a sister[142] as a wife,
One day shall crown the alliance on 't,[143] so please you,
Here at my house and at my proper[144] cost.

DUKE

Madam, I am most apt[145] to embrace your offer.   300
[*To* VIOLA] Your master quits you;[146] and for your service
   done him,
So much against the mettle[147] of your sex,
So far beneath your soft and tender breeding,[148]
And since you called me master for so long,
Here is my hand; you shall from this time be   305
Your master's mistress.[149]

OLIVIA

A sister! You are she.

243

150 *must not* – "cannot".
151 *from it* – "differently".
152 *hand* – "handwriting".
153 *phrase* – "style".
154 *your invention* – "composed by yourself".
155 *the modesty of honour* – "honourably and without deceit".
156 *lighter* – "less important".
157 *acting this* – "when I acted on this".
158 *suffered* – "caused".
159 *geck* – "idiot".
160 *invention* – "trickery".
161 *the character* – "my way of forming letters".

Re-enter FABIAN, *with* MALVOLIO

DUKE

Is this the madman?

OLIVIA

Ay, my lord, this same.
How now, Malvolio?

MALVOLIO

Madam, you have done me wrong,
Notorious wrong.

OLIVIA

Have I, Malvolio? No.   310

MALVOLIO

Lady, you have. Pray you peruse that letter.
You must not[150] now deny it is your hand;
Write from it,[151] if you can, in hand[152] or phrase;[153]
Or say 't is not your seal nor your invention;[154]
You can say none of this. Well, grant it then,   315
And tell me, in the modesty of honour,[155]
Why you have given me such clear lights of favour,
Bade me come smiling and cross-gartered to you,
To put on yellow stockings, and to frown
Upon Sir Toby and the lighter[156] people;   320
And, acting this[157] in an obedient hope,
Why have you suffered[158] me to be imprisoned,
Kept in a dark house, visited by the priest,
And made the most notorious geck[159] and gull
That e'er invention[160] played on? Tell me why.   325

OLIVIA

Alas, Malvolio, this is not my writing,
Though, I confess, much like the character;[161]
But, out of question, 't is Maria's hand;

245

162 *I do bethink me* – "I recall".
163 *cam'st* – "you came".
164 *in such . . . thee* – "behaving in such ways as you were advised here".
165 *This practice . . . thee* – "this joke has been played upon you most cruelly".
166 *grounds and authors* – "reasons and makers".
167 *to come* – "in the future".
168 *Upon . . . him* – "because of the proud and impolite behaviour we disliked in him".
169 *writ* – "wrote".
170 *at Sir Toby's great importance* – "as a result of Sir Toby's strong persuasion".

171 *it was followed* – "it (the trick) was played".
172 *May rather pluck on* – "will more likely cause".
173 *baffled thee* – "made you look a fool".
174 *thrown.* Here the word actually used in the letter was *thrust* (see II.v.124).
175 *I was . . . interlude* – "I had a part, sir, in this little play".
176 *the whirligig of time* – "time, like a spinning top", which changes circumstances as it spins round. Feste has just mentioned a situation where Malvolio made him look foolish (I.v.72–7); now Feste has his revenge.

And now I do bethink me,[162] it was she
First told me thou wast mad; then cam'st [163] in smiling,   330
And in such forms which here were presupposed
Upon thee[164] in the letter. Prithee, be content;
This practice hath most shrewdly passed upon thee;[165]
But when we know the grounds and authors[166] of it,
Thou shalt be both the plaintiff and the judge   335
Of thine own cause.

FABIAN

      Good madam, hear me speak,
And let no quarrel nor no brawl to come[167]
Taint the condition of this present hour,
Which I have wondered at. In hope it shall not,
Most freely I confess, myself and Toby   340
Set this device against Malvolio here,
Upon some stubborn and uncourteous parts
We had conceived against him.[168] Maria writ[169]
The letter at Sir Toby's great importance;[170]
In recompense whereof he hath married her.   345
How with a sportful malice it was followed,[171]
May rather pluck on[172] laughter than revenge,
If that the injuries be justly weighed
That have on both sides passed.

OLIVIA

Alas, poor fool, how have they baffled thee![173]   350

FESTE

Why, "some are born great, some achieve greatness, and some
have greatness thrown[174] upon them". I was one, sir, in this
interlude;[175] one Sir Topas, sir; but that's all one [*Imitating*
MALVOLIO] "By the Lord, fool, I am not mad." But do you remember? "Madam, why laugh you at such a barren rascal? An 355
you smile not, he's gagged"; and thus the whirligig of time[176]
brings in his revenges.

177 *entreat . . . peace* – "beg earnestly for peace".

178 *golden time convents* – "the happy time suits".

179 *combination* – "union", in marriage.

180 *dear* – "precious".

181 *so*, i.e. called by this name.

182 *habits* – "dress".

183 *Sings . . .* This song, which Feste sings to the audience when all the other characters have left the stage, has a delightful rhythm, but, on the surface at least, little meaning. It seems to suggest that real life, as it passes, is a serious matter and quite different from that of the comedy we have just seen.

184 *When that I was and* – "When I was"; "that" and "and" in the first line of the song have no separate meaning; neither has the phrase *hey, ho*, which occurs throughout the song, and was often used in songs of Shakespeare's time.

185 *toy* – something unworthy of consideration; his foolery was regarded simply as childishness.

186 *man's estate* – "manhood"; then, apparently, men shut their gates in his face because of his misdeeds.

187 *wive* – "take a wife".

188 *By swaggering . . . thrive* – "I could not do well by boasting".

But when in other habits[182] you are seen
Orsino's mistress, and his fancy's queen

MALVOLIO

I 'll be revenged on the whole pack of you.

[*Exit*

OLIVIA

He hath been most notoriously abused.

DUKE

Pursue him, and entreat him to a peace.[177]   360
He hath not told us of the captain yet;
When that is known, and golden time convents,[178]
A solemn combination[179] shall be made
Of our dear[180] souls. Meantime, sweet sister,
We will not part from hence. Cesario, come;   365
For so[181] you shall be, while you are a man;
But when in other habits[182] you are seen,
Orsino's mistress, and his fancy's queen.

[*Exeunt all except* FESTE

FESTE

[*Sings*][183]   *When that I was and*[184] *a little tiny boy,*
      With hey, ho, the wind and the rain;   370
    A foolish thing was but a toy,[185]
     For the rain it raineth every day.

    But when I came to man's estate,[186]
     With hey, ho, the wind and the rain;
    'Gainst knaves and thieves men shut their gate,   375
     For the rain it raineth every day.

    But when I came, alas, to wive,[187]
     With hey, ho, the wind and the rain;
    By swaggering[188] *could I never thrive,*
     For the rain it raineth every day.   380

249

189 *unto my beds* – (perhaps) " to the end of my life".

190 *toss-pots* – "drunkards".

191 *begun* for *began*.

192 *that's all one* – a phrase which has already been used twice in this scene, by Sir Toby at line 183, and by Feste himself at 353.

But when I came unto my beds,[189]
  With hey, ho, the wind and the rain;
With toss-pots[190] still had drunken heads,
  For the rain it raineth every day.   385

A great while ago the world begun,[191]
  With hey, ho, the wind and the rain;
But that's all one,[192] our play is done,
  And we'll strive to please you every day.
                                        [Exit

SOME ADVICE FOR EXAMINATION CANDIDATES

Begin your examination by reading through the question-paper slowly and thoughtfully. Then decide on which of the questions you will answer. Make sure you have chosen the right number of questions, and that they come from the right sections of the paper.

Do exactly what the questions ask you to do. Plan each of your answers carefully before you begin to write them out in full. All the time, check to make absolutely sure you are answering the questions themselves, and not writing about something else.

Questions on Shakespeare fall into a number of different types. Your teachers will be able to tell you which of these types are most likely to be set in the examination you are taking. In what follows, we have identified five main types of question. We give an illustration of each type, and with it some suggestions as to how it might best be answered.

1. You are given *some short passages* from the play and asked to answer questions on them. Such questions usually refer only to the passage itself and its immediate context. Choose the passages you know best. Make certain you answer every question set on the passage you choose.

For example:

This is the air; that is the glorious sun;
This pearl she gave me, I do feel't and see't;
And though 't is wonder that enwraps me thus,
Yet 't is not madness.

(i) Who says this? To whom? At what point in the play?
(ii) How would you tell the person concerned to speak and act out these lines so as to bring out their full significance?

(Welsh Joint Education Committee, GCE Ordinary Level, Summer 1984.)

SUGGESTED ANSWER

(The passage quoted is at the beginning of IV.iii, p.209 in NEW SWAN.)

(i) Sebastian.
    To himself.

253

Olivia, believing that Sebastian is "Cesario", has broken up a quarrel between him and Sir Toby, and has then taken him to her own house, greatly to his surprise. She wants to be married to him and has gone to get a priest to conduct the wedding ceremony without delay.

(ii) Speak the lines slowly and deliberately, making them support the sort of wide-eyed amazement which Sebastian must be experiencing as stranger and stranger things begin happening to him. Make these lines, and the rest of the speech which follows them, affirm that what you experience is amazement, not madness. You must therefore speak confidently, showing that you trust your senses: you look up to the sky and down to the pearl which Olivia has just given you.

2. You are given *a longer passage* and have to answer questions on it. The passage may be printed in full on the examination paper; or you may be given a plain text of the play to use. If you are to use a plain text, make absolutely sure you find the right lines in it.

Questions on a longer passage generally refer both to details in the passage itself, and to its setting in the play as a whole, not just its immediate surroundings. You may be asked, for instance, about the function of the passage in what it reveals about a character's personality, or about some features of its style and the significance of these features, or about how situations presented in the passage are resolved as the play proceeds.

For example:
You are given the passage I.i.32–40 (p.3 in NEW SWAN), and have to answer questions relating to it as follows.
(i) What has caused Orsino to make this speech?
(ii) To what does 'the rich golden shaft' refer? Why are 'liver, brains and heart' mentioned by Orsino?
(iii) How true are Orsino's predictions about Olivia? What element of irony do they eventually turn out to contain?
(Southern Universities' Joint Board, GCE Ordinary Level, 1985.)

SUGGESTED ANSWER
(i) Orsino is in love with Olivia, but has just heard that she will not see him because she is in deep mourning for her brother, who has re-

254

cently died. She says she will keep her brother's memory fresh by mourning her loss for seven years. In this speech Orsino says, in effect: If she can love a dead brother so devotedly, how will she love when the right man woos and wins her as his wife?

(ii) The "rich golden shaft" refers to the arrow of the little love god Cupid. He was thought of as shooting such arrows at random, and when one of these arrows hit a person, that person fell in love.

Orsino mentions "liver, brains and heart" because these organs of the body were taken as "seats", i.e. the proper locations, of human qualities: passions in the liver, judgement in the brain, and affections in the heart. He looks forward to a time when Olivia's love for him will "fill" all these "seats".

(iii) Orsino's predictions about Olivia are true to the extent that she does indeed fall deeply in love with someone else. This is sexual love, which is different from the *debt of love* she vowed to pay to her dead brother, but both are called *love*. Orsino is wrong in implying that he will be the man to win Olivia's heart. She falls in love instead with his messenger, Viola, whom he believes to be a man, "Cesario".

The irony of his predictions lies in his mention of *one self king*. Taken literally, this means "one king only", i.e. any man Olivia falls in love with who will rule her affections. We all know, however, that Orsino is talking about himself, even if he does not say this. The element of irony is the contrast between the literal meaning, which he is right about (Olivia does fall in love like this), and the implied meaning, which he is *not* right about (she does not fall in love with him).

3. You are asked to write an essay on certain *aspects of a single character, or a number of characters,* in the play. Your task is to write about the character(s) from a particular point of view, not just to tell their story or the story of the play.

For example:
By referring to his appearances throughout the play, outline the stages in the downfall of Malvolio. Show in your account which defects in his character contribute to his downfall.
(Welsh Joint Education Committee, GCE Ordinary Level, Summer 1984.)

The first part of this question, about the "stages in the downfall of Malvolio", makes it necessary for you to think through the play and note down each of these "stages" as you remember them. These notes are an essential preparation for writing the sort of answer your examiners are asking for. Do not begin writing your final answer straight away, because if you do you may miss out important stages in Malvolio's progress through the play.

Next, indicate by the side of each of your notes on these "stages" what particular defect they can be associated with. You will now have a good plan to build your full answer on. You can write this by filling out your notes, and making them complete sentences which explain in detail what you want to say. Do not leave it to the examiners to work out what you have in mind; write enough to show you have the precise knowledge and understanding of the play needed to answer this question.

Your notes on the "stages" might be on the following lines. (We have included scene references to help you, but these of course would not be required in the examination.)

— By Olivia's side as her steward, he does not enjoy Feste's clowning. He has no sense of humour. She sends him after Viola with a message and a ring. He does exactly what he is told by Olivia, but how much does he understand it? Has he any imagination? (I.v, II.ii).

— He tries to quieten the members of Olivia's household when they are drinking together but it is obvious he has no good authority over them, either through his office or his personality. (II.iii).

— He finds Maria's fake letter; he has some doubts about it but in the end accepts it as genuine. It fits in well with his own dreams of glory as Olivia's husband. He fantasises. (II.v).

— He now behaves strangely in front of Olivia, and has dressed strangely too, exactly as Maria's letter told him to do. He is provoked by Sir Toby and the rest. He shows again he has no imagination, and is so self-important that he cannot see when he is being made fun of. (III.iv). Olivia has doubts about his sanity, but says he is valuable to her as a servant. (III.iv.57).

— He is put in a dark room, and cruelly baited by Feste. At last he is able to write a letter to Olivia, telling her how he has been wronged, but only after promising to reward Feste for bringing him pen, paper and a light. He understands trading better than merrymaking. (IV.ii).

— His letter persuades Olivia that he is not mad, and Fabian and the

256

others admit they have tricked him. He cannot join in the general fun at the end of the play, but thinks only of revenge on those who have played their ugly joke on him. (V.i.).

(The note about him in this book, pp. xvii–xviii, will give you some further ideas in connection with this question.)

4. Examiners often set some questions which relate to *the play as a whole*. They may ask you about a major aspect of the play; or they may quote something a critic has written about it, and then ask you to comment on this quotation.

For example:
Choose *two* letters that are sent in *Twelfth Night,* and describe briefly what the letters contain. Then show how the letters themselves, and the situations they give rise to, are amusing to the audience.
(Welsh Joint Education Committee, GCE Ordinary Level, Summer 1984.)

Taken at face value, this question may not sound very difficult. There are only three letters in the plot of *Twelfth Night,* and each one of them is memorable in the part it plays. But on the other hand a very precise knowledge of them, and the situations they give rise to, is required if this question is to be answered adequately. You are asked to write also on why the audience finds the letters and their consequences amusing.

In the notes which follow, we have selected for special study the letters composed by Sir Toby and Maria, to be read by Malvolio (II.v.79ff.); and the one written by Sir Andrew as a challenge to "Cesario" (III.iv.129ff.). Notice how these suggestions for an answer break up the question point by point, and deal with each part in turn; this is the way to ensure that all the details are given as required.

The letter in II.v has been prepared by Sir Toby and his companions in Olivia's household, and written by Maria in Olivia's hand so as to deceive Malvolio into thinking that Olivia is in love with him. They all agree in disliking him for being self-important and overbearing in the way he treats them.

This letter begins with two verses which could be read to mean that the writer has a secret love she will not declare except by writing four letters to indicate the loved-one. These are M, O, A and I, all of which are in

257

Malvolio's name. The rest of the letter is in prose. It appears to tell Malvolio that Olivia would be pleased if he behaved more boldly towards her kinsmen and servants, because he is destined for great things if he does so. If he acts like an important man, with his own individual habits and dress, he will rise above his fellow-servants and, by marrying her, become master of the household.

The second letter we have chosen (III.iv.129ff.) contains a challenge prepared by Sir Andrew and addressed to "Cesario", i.e. the disguised Viola whom Olivia has fallen in love with. It is a crude and unexplained threat, on the lines that because "Cesario" is treated kindly by Olivia, Sir Andrew is jealous of "him" and will attack "him" on his way home. They will then fight to the death.

The first letter takes Malvolio in completely. When he finds it, he is already day-dreaming about what might happen if he and Olivia could be married. Even though the message in the letter is not at all clear, he takes it as confirming that Olivia is in love with him, and doing this quickly leads to his downfall. He begins to behave and dress in the ways suggested in the letter. Olivia thinks he is mad, and tells Sir Toby to look after him; he is imprisoned in a dark room and baited by Feste. Eventually he is able to write to Olivia, referring to what he took to be her letter to him. All is then explained, but he can only threaten revenge on those who wanted to punish him for his proud behaviour to them.

All this is amusing, despite its serious undertones as to the treatment of a suspected madman, because we feel that the self-important and over-ambitious Malvolio has had a good confidence-trick played on him, and his character, so lacking in any sense of humour, is an ideal target for anyone who enjoys the funny side of life. We laugh primarily because he is too serious to realise that a trick is being played on him.

The second letter is different in many ways. It never reaches "Cesario", the person it is addressed to, because Sir Toby, who at first offered to deliver it, decides not to because it is so foolish that it will not be taken seriously. Instead, he acts as a go-between urging on both Sir Andrew and "Cesario" to fight one another.

The fun lies in Sir Andrew thinking his letter is good and coherent, when it is not; and also in the way Sir Andrew is so pleased with what he has written. Indeed the dialogue here, when the others congratulate him on how well he has written the letter, as well as his own obvious satisfaction, add to the comedy. It must be admitted, though, that, like Malvolio, Sir Andrew is a victim of self-deception, which it is perhaps not quite right to laugh at. The results of both situations are harsh: as Malvolio is treated like a madman, Sir Andrew and Sir Toby suffer badly from the fight with Sebastian, not the "Cesario" whom the challenge was prepared for.

5. Your teachers may have been working with you mainly on producing the play for the stage. If so, you will be getting good advice from them on what you are likely to be asked in your examination. However, you may find the following hints useful, not only for the details they contain, but also for the arrangement of the material which they suggest. You may expect questions to be on the following lines:

> Imagine you are working on a production of *Twelfth Night*. How would you direct one particular scene. (The scene may be prescribed, or you may be free to choose it for yourself.) What especially would you want to convey to your audience in this part of the play?

In planning your answer, you need to visualise as precisely as you can what has to happen on the stage, i.e. what the essentials are as they are given in the written text. Begin by writing down some rough notes about these essentials so that you keep them in your mind while you consider what you would do as director. Do *not* write out the story of the play or the scene you have chosen to work on. Just indicate briefly the particular points in the dialogue or action you are dealing with, and the examiners will know what you are referring to.

We have chosen I.v to illustrate the approach we have in mind, and we note below some aspects of this scene which you will have to consider in producing it for the stage. Under each heading you will find some suggestions and questions to think about. You can build up an appropriate answer by developing the suggestions and answering the questions in relation to the production you visualise.

A lot happens in this scene, much of it crucial to the development of the plot. It is therefore very important that your audience understands what is happening and gets a strong impression of the focal points in it.

The stage set

There is a lot of movement, and Olivia's room must therefore be big enough to accommodate it easily. Olivia herself dominates and needs to be placed accordingly. Would you like to place her on an important-looking chair with a high back, raised a little from the other furniture? Or would you prefer to make her stand out by the use of lighting? A table in front of her might help the actress who plays her to hit the right formal pose, like a person sitting in judgement. Of course the furniture and fittings will have to look grand, because Olivia is a great lady. You will need plenty of open space for Malvolio to stand in, away from all the rest but at Olivia's side, and also to some degree looking as if he is also in judgement. Generous space is needed too for Feste and Maria at the beginning, and for Viola when she is brought in.

Costumes and make-up

The first appearances of both Olivia and Malvolio are in this scene. Olivia is in mourning and will have to be in black, but still look young and attractive. Her mourning dress will naturally have a veil which she can easily bring into play (145) and later lift away from her face (203).

Malvolio is also to be dressed soberly and quietly, so that the contrast with him in yellow stockings and cross-gartered (III.iv) is the more striking.

How can you make Feste, in his clown's costume, look bedraggled and in disgrace, and yet bright enough to be a source of wit?

We have already seen Viola dressed as a young man (I.iv) but you may want her to seem more noticeable or attractive here, perhaps by the use of a different make-up.

Lighting

This scene hardly calls for any special lighting effects to draw your audience's attention away from one group of actors on the stage to another. If you believe this is so, a suitable arrangement may be to have your main floodlighting directed from one side of the stage, as if it comes through a great chamber window on the sunny side of Olivia's house.

Movement

There is a lot of movement in this scene and it has to be planned carefully so that the flow of the action is not obscured or confused. One way of presenting this is to split the scene up into episodes, and, by drawing plans of your stage, show where your actors will be for each episode. You will need to use both sides of the stage for your exits and entrances, so that (e.g.) Maria comes in from one side at 85, and Viola (146) at another. When Sir Toby comes in, his movements must show he is "half drunk" (101); his movements should not be exaggerated, however.

For the purposes of arranging the movement, the "episodes" could be identified as follows:

1) 1–30   Maria and Feste.
2) 31–85   Olivia and Malvolio, etc. join Feste.
3) 86–100   News comes of "Cesario" at the gate.
4) 101–121   Sir Toby, half drunk, in from the gate.
5) 122–144   Malvolio reports on "Cesario's" arrival.
6) 145–190   "Cesario" arrives.
7) 191–266   "Cesario" alone with Olivia.
8) 266–end   Malvolio ordered to go after "Cesario".

Speech
Do you find any parts of the scene which call for variations in the speed at which the words are spoken? You might consider that Feste's rather long speech at 37–46 could best be taken rather quickly; it is not particularly interesting because it depends on styles of word-play which are not current in English today. For the rest, you might try to decide on a suitable pace for the spoken language in each episode to be taken at. A lot of material consists of quick exchanges, where the pace must never be allowed to slacken.

Decide on points in the scene which you like specially emphasised; Olivia's opinion of Malvolio at 78 might be one. Another may be Malvolio's literal reporting of his conversation with "Cesario" at the gate (122–136); is he really being literal, or does even he penetrate to the humour of "he ['Cesario'] seems to have a foreknowledge of that too"? He will have to adjust his voice accordingly.

A good deal can, and we think should, be made of "Cesario's" poetic lines at 235–243, rising to a dramatic peak at "Cry out 'Olivia!'" Should she draw in her breath with amazement when she sees Olivia's face (204)?

Sound effects

Do you want to bring in any special effects? The sounds at Olivia's gate are *not* called for because in such a great house the main entrance would be too far away from the great chambers to be within earshot.

These are, then, just suggestions and questions; many more will come to your mind as you work on the play. However, when you write out your answer fair for the examination, and prepare your sketch-plans, you will not be able to record everything you have to decide on and resolve in your production. Using the scheme of headings shown above should help you to arrange your main topics effectively, and bring them within reasonable limits.

Alternatively, you may prefer to give an account of your production in sequence, episode by episode, as words are spoken and things happen in the play. Even so, the headings set out above will help you to cover the various aspects of presentation which go to make up a performance in the theatre.

262